COACH'S CHALLENGE

COACH'S CHALLENGE

FAITH, FOOTBALL,

AND FILLING THE FATHER GAP

MIKE GOTTFRIED

WITH
RON BENSON

HOWARD BOOKS

A DIVISION OF SIMON & SCHUSTER

New York   London   Toronto   Sydney

Our purpose at Howard Books is to:

- *Increase faith* in the hearts of growing Christians
- *Inspire holiness* in the lives of believers
- *Instill hope* in the hearts of struggling people everywhere

Because He's coming again!

 Published by Howard Books, a division of Simon & Schuster, Inc.
1230 Avenue of the Americas, New York, NY 10020
www.howardpublishing.com

Library of Congress Cataloging-in-Publication Data

Gottfried, Mike.
    Coach's challenge : faith, football, and filling the father gap / Mike Gottfried with
Ron Benson.
    p. cm.
    Summary: "Presents the life experiences that molded ESPN college football analyst
Mike Gottfried into a strong advocate for fatherless boys and chronicles his time
coaching Murray State, Cincinnati, Kansas, and Pitt"—Provided by publisher.
    1. Gottfried, Mike. 2. Football coaches—United States—Biography. 3. Broad-
casters—United States—Biography. 4. Television broadcasting of sports—United
States. 5. Boys—United States—Conduct of life. 6. Fatherless families—United
States. 7. Sports—Religious aspects. I. Benson, Ron. II. Title.
    GV939.G67A3 2007
    796.332092—dc22
    [B]
                                                                    2007010603

ISBN-13: 978-1-4165-4355-8
ISBN-10:   1-4165-4355-4

10 9 8 7 6 5 4 3 2 1

For information regarding special discounts for bulk purchases,
please contact: Simon & Schuster Special Sales at 1-800-456-6798
or business@simonandschuster.com.

Edited by Steve Halliday
Cover design by Jason Gabbert
Interior design by Jaime Putorti

CONTENTS

To my father, Frederick (Fritz) John Gottfried
He was a loving father.
In the short time we had together he gave me what
a son needs. He gave me affection, affirmation,
acceptance, attention, and provided loving
authority.
Thanks, Dad!

ACKNOWLEDGMENTS

Football is a team sport and so it was in bringing forth this book. There were many valuable teammates!

Thank you Mike Atkins for bringing forth the vision for a book, and for the many other opportunities I have experienced since I met you. You are an encourager, friend, and a man of integrity.

Thank you Ron Benson for the collaboration on this book. Working with you has been a pleasure. I appreciate your diligence in getting all of the story written down.

Thank you Steve Halliday for the excellent job of editing.

Thank you to Howard Publishing for helping me share my vision.

Thank you to Denny and Philis Boultinghouse. Our prayers have been and will always be with you.

Thank you Rey Dempsey for your wise counsel, prayer, and teaching. I appreciate the friend and mentor you have been to me. You have been consistent and constant in my life.

Thank you John Erickson for the many times you have

given me your time and wisdom. Your guidance and support have been important to me in pursuing the call on my life.

Thank you Monte Johnson. You have been a wonderful example to me and so consistent in encouraging and supporting me. I appreciate all you have done!

Rocky Alt, my hometown friend. We now stand together in the gap for many young men who have experienced the same missing part in their lives as we have. Thank you for standing with me and working diligently for this cause.

Thank you to my wife and best friend, Mickey. Without you none of this would be possible. I love you so much. And to my precious daughters, Mindy and Marcy. You are jewels in my life.

To my loyal and loving brothers, Joe and John, thank you for always being there.

To the people of Crestline, Ohio, where my life began, I say thank you for providing for me, my wife, and so many others a community that was a great environment in which to grow up and be nurtured. A place where people cared and worked together.

My heart is full of gratitude for all those in my life, not listed here, who mentored me and filled the father-gap. You made it possible for me to move into the destiny God had planned for me. Jeremiah 29:11.

WHAT ARE YOU DOING HERE?

My heart thumped from excitement and anticipation as I walked into the White House. I could hardly believe it! Here I was, entering the home of the president of the United States of America. The arrangements had all been made, the time for our official appointment had come. It was truly amazing.

So, of course, at precisely that moment, the loud opening fanfare for ESPN sports came jangling from my pocket—the ringtone for my cell phone.

I felt a little embarrassed that I hadn't turned the thing off, but I hardly ever do. I stopped our little procession of guests, took out the phone, and looked at the screen to check the caller ID. If it had been from anyone else—an NCAA coach, a ball-player, someone from ESPN—I would have flipped the off switch and not taken the call. Whoever it was could wait and call me later.

But it was from one of my boys, Andy.

I looked at the guard at the gate, turned around to my entourage, and said, "Hold on just a minute. I've gotta take this call." And White House security personnel and the people with me waited while I talked to Andy.

"Hey, Andy. How are you doing?"

"Coach! Where you at?" My boys always ask me that question, because I could be anywhere. They like the idea that they can call me anywhere, whether I'm in some big city or in a small town of some state they've never visited. In my work as an ESPN college football commentator, I cover eighteen games a season, so I travel a lot.

"I'm getting ready to walk into the White House," I said.

"*No*. You're kidding me! Where you at, really?" I had a hard time convincing Andy of the truth.

"I'm at the White House," I insisted. "I'm gonna talk to Laura Bush's people."

"*Really?* Laura Bush? You really there?" He still sounded skeptical.

"That's right. I'm right here at the gate, ready to go in."

"What are you doing there?"

His question caught me up short. Without knowing it, Andy had asked me exactly the right question. *What* am *I doing here?* I began thinking. *How did I end up at the White House with an invitation to speak with staffers for Laura Bush? How did all of this happen?*

One thing was for sure: I wasn't there because of sports. I love sports—I always have—and I've been both a player and a coach. I get to talk about college football on ESPN every Saturday during the season, and I make good money for doing so. You could say I live sports. But that's not what drives me. It's not my passion—at least, not anymore. I had not come to the White House because of my connection to sports.

I was there for the boys.

Through my work with Team Focus, I take personal responsibility for more than six hundred boys who share one thing in common: they lack a functional father. I know them all by name and they know me. They live all over the country, from Washington, D.C., to Los Angeles, from Detroit to Mobile. They all have my cell phone number and my toll-free office number, and they all know they can call me, any time of the day or night, and I'll be there. I *will* answer.

Today I got eleven calls, all of them from boys ranging in age from ten to seventeen. Eleven calls is about average for me in one day. I always take their calls, because if they had dads, their dads would answer. But since they don't, I answer.

Visualize with me for a moment. Take a picture of your family, an old-fashioned family portrait. You have your grandmother, looking a little serious. Your grandfather is there, with that stiff, little smile of his. Your mom is standing in front of you because just last year you got an inch of height on her. Your brothers and sisters are there, some down in front, some behind you. And your father is in there, standing just to your left. He has his big, firm hand on your shoulder and a big smile on his face, brimming with satisfied, whole-some pride.

As you visualize that family portrait—watch as your grand-mother fades away, out of the picture, leaving behind a light gray space in her shape. That's only natural; it happens that way. People die. Imagine the same thing with your grandpa. He was pretty old, so you expect it.

But now imagine that your dad—young and vigorous, his hands touching you with affection and affirmation—just fades away, too. In his place stands a gap, a hole, in the exact shape of your dad. It's the only thing left behind when he disappears from the picture. He leaves is an open and vulnerable spot.

You simply can't replace a father. No substitute can com-pletely fill in that faded place in the picture—it's impossible. It's too broad a gap, too immense an absence. Still, those of us who have lost our dads have a great thirst to fill that hole with something or someone. That thirst drives us, whether or not we realize it. It compels us to make a decision. It is that deci-sion—what to use to fill the gap—that makes all the difference in the life of a fatherless boy. While no living human being can take the place of a father, a good sub is better than a bad one any day.

I wrote this book because I want to tell you the story of how God prepared me ahead of time for the plans he has worked out in my life. I want to tell you about my experiences and about our work with Team Focus and how we try to fill the gap for some fatherless boys.

But do you want to know my real purpose in telling my

story? It's to coach you off your couch and into God's plans for you. In other words, I want to ask you Andy's question:

What are you doing here?

If the hole left by your father still sits empty in your own heart, I want you to know that someone understands exactly how you feel. Whether you're reading this book because you are interested in my story, or because you are interested in the needs of fatherless boys, I want you to know that you, too, can help fill the gap in the life of some young man. And it all begins with asking yourself a question:

What am I doing here?

COACH'S CHALLENGE

CHAPTER ONE

GROWING UP
IN CRESTLINE

As a boy growing up in Crestline, Ohio, the furthest thing from my mind was visiting the White House. My little hometown provided me with a happy and peaceful life. I had the childhood every kid should enjoy.

Crestline was home, and it always will be. Whenever I go back there, even though today I live in Mobile, Alabama, I always say, "I'm going home." In a lot of small towns you hear people say, "I can't wait to get out of this place." Not in Crestline! Most of the time, people from my hometown say, "I can't wait to get back home." When I was young, neighborhood friends might travel on vacation to Chicago or New York or other places, but the kids couldn't wait to get back to Crestline.

1

My own family sometimes went out of town, too. Maybe we'd travel to West Virginia or to a nearby lake. My brothers and I enjoyed all those trips—but not for long. We soon became impatient to hurry back to Crestline. As fun and adventurous as some of those places might have seemed, we all thought Crestline offered even more fun and adventure. It was always great.

When my wife, Mickey, and I drive by my boyhood home today, I'll say to her, "That was a time where everything was good. There was no sadness, no pain, no anything—just *great.*" We drive by the old house or the elementary school or the baseball field, and the pleasant memories fill my head. When I remember my life up through the age of ten, just one phrase comes to mind: *it was all good.*

U.S. 30, the Lincoln Highway, runs through my hometown on its long way from California to New York. Crestline used to be a big stop on the way east or west, but that's not the reason I consider it such a remarkable place. No, it's the memories of a hometown that make it special. Good memories of Crestline come back to me again and again, because God continues to use that town and the people in it to shape my destiny.

My hometown provided the training ground for what was to come in my life, preparing me for the future. It's amazing to look back and see how so many of the things that made Crestline so great are now sewn into the fabric of my life. In God's plans for me, Crestline was the first stop along the tracks. The people of my small town were God's tools for growing me, training me, preparing me. Crestline was like a practice field,

God was the coach, and solid moral values were the lesson of the day.

Those values included hard work, respect and caring for people, discipline and independence, playing as a team and playing fair, and the importance of family. In all of the varied activities of life in our small town, I learned those lessons continually.

We were South Side people. From the day I knew anything, I knew I was on the South Side team. The railroad lines intersected at the center of town, and informal teams of boys formed in the four sections. When we'd go to the park to play ball, we played against the West Enders, the North End, and the East End. We were the South Siders.

We South Siders were the kids from the poor side of town, and that meant we were the perpetual underdogs. So naturally we earned a tough-kid reputation. Our song said it all about us:

> *We are the gang from Southside you hear so much about.*
> *Most people laugh and stare at us whenever we go out.*
> *We're not stuck-up at all about the stupid things we do.*
> *Most all the people hate our guts; we hope that you do, too.*

Life was about being on a team. What I know about teams—the way they function and the way God can use them—started in Crestline.

The Little South Siders team got its recruits from elementary-age kids. Older boys made up the Big South Siders team. While I was on the Little team, my brother Joe was on the Big team. His group went around to the local merchants and got them to spring for nice gray jerseys with red trim. The jerseys gave the boys an identity, and having that kind of identity is important to any kid.

As a team, we did everything on our own; no adults were involved—at least, not much. Most of our dads traveled with the railroads, so we'd coach ourselves and ump ourselves. We did it all. When he wasn't working, my dad would help put some games together or referee from behind the pitcher's mound. But he didn't do it so much because we needed him as that he wanted to be there. Coach Hutson, the unofficial "town coach" (you'll hear more about him later), also helped us a lot with every sport we played. But we did most of it on our own.

Hamilton Park was our turf, the park on our side of town, the South Side. That's where the football stadium was, just a few yards down the road from our house. An old archway marked the entrance into the park. Up the hill there was a goldfish pond and beyond that, the ball fields. A large stone monument sat on top of the hill—a big rock, with a circle of smaller rocks. Every time I went up to the park, I tried to climb it, but I could never get up there. That all the other kids *could* do it just made me try harder.

The football stadium sat on the flats at the top of the park. I loved it there. I'd sit and look at the grass and the bleachers and dream, *Someday I'm gonna play football for a college team*. The smell of grass still makes me smile.

The tennis courts were a new addition back then, although we didn't play much tennis. Instead, we used the courts for Wiffle ball. We had big competitions to knock the ball out of the fences surrounding the court, pretending we were hitting them out of Cleveland Stadium.

The South Siders sometimes got a trip together to travel to Cleveland for Batboy Night with the Indians. On that night, kids came from all around to try out for a batboy position. We would write to the Indians ahead of time for free tickets, then we'd get a bunch of boys together and take the train to the big city. It cost us $4.02 for everything, something we'd have to save up for, but it was worth it. After the game we'd move over to the arcade and play pinball, or make a record, or get our pictures taken in the little booth. Being there gave us a certain amount of independence, and it gave me confidence.

No adult accompanied us to the games. That may sound strange today, but back then it was okay, even a normal thing. It was just us and about seventy thousand fans at that huge stadium. I loved being in a stadium like that with all the people cheering the home team and enjoying the game. It remains one of the greatest thrills in the world to me.

At the very center of Crestline, two rail lines come together and cross. In my boyhood days, the Pennsylvania Railroad came through town roughly east/west, dividing the town north and south. The north/south line of the New York Central Railroad, nicknamed the Big Four, divided the town east and west. In those days the roads took a backseat in importance to the trains.

Things are different today. Now, two tracks meet unnoticed under a highway overpass. But back in 1954, at the intersection of those lines, Crestline moved day and night like a living thing, a beehive of activity. People came and went, traveling in all directions. At least thirty passenger trains rumbled through town every day, about one every fifteen minutes during peak hours. Freight trains came through even more frequently. The Crestline Roundhouse became famous for the volume of trains that got serviced there. Crestline was a railroad town through and through.

Nearly everyone in town either worked for the railroad or in some way made a living by the railroad. A person could make more on the railroad than teaching, so some teachers quit their jobs and found work on the tracks. A sheriff in Bucyrus, a neighboring town, quit his job to work for the railroad. And why not? The railroad was a pretty good place to work. If a man worked hard, he could make good money and get some good benefits for his family. No one growing up in Crestline could avoid learning about a good work ethic, since it was on display every day.

Businesses sprouted up all over the city to feed, house, and entertain both passengers and workers on the trains. Frequent trains meant people could get off one train, do some business or shopping, and catch another one a short while later. Crestline made a living because of the trains, and we used the railroad to our advantage any way we could.

Some entrepreneurial boys found a way to make a few dollars from the train passengers. Except for engines going to the yard, the trains didn't stay in Crestline for more than five or ten minutes, just enough time for passengers to gather their things and get on or off. My buddies made sandwiches—usually bologna or ham wrapped in paper—and went into the trains, selling sandwiches for a dime. They'd walk through the train and ask, "You want to buy a sandwich?" They'd get off the train just before it left for the next stop.

The boy businessmen soon discovered that, since they weren't on the train for long, they could leave off the meat. So they'd ask, "Do you want ketchup or mustard on your sandwich?" If a customer said, "Ketchup," that's what he'd get: a ketchup sandwich. Same with mustard.

Every once in a while the boys would get stuck on the train until the next station, and then they'd either hide or try to talk their way out of trouble. That worked fine until a group of servicemen came by in a troop train. The sandwich sales were good—so good that one guy, Jimmy, stayed on the train too late to hop off. He had to go on to the next station, and that meant he was traveling with a bunch of angry servicemen who didn't much care for meatless sandwiches. They caught up to him and worked him over pretty good. Eventually the police caught wind of the goings-on and put an end to the ketchup-sandwich operation. So in the end, everyone got a lesson in the value of honest labor—yet another lesson from the trains.

Since my house and the houses of all my friends were on the other side of the tracks from the school, we had to cross the tracks at least twice a day, ten or twelve of them lined up together. We'd leave early in the morning to allow for long trains that sometimes got stalled. If trains from both lines were waiting to move through, it would be a long time before we could cross.

A manned and heated switching shanty stood right where the tracks crossed. On cold days we ducked into it. Tom, one of my uncles, worked as a guard there, and he'd let us in. But since you could fit only Uncle Tom and one other person in the shanty, sometimes we took turns.

Across the tracks stood the old station, with businesses and restaurants and apartments hanging over the corner and going down the street. A big clock on the front of the building gave engineers the exact time. Our whole town set time by that clock—but it was the comings and goings of the railroad that determined the life rhythms of our whole town. As I look back, I know God used the trains to mold my life.

Railroad schedules even played a part in the church we attended. In Crestline, there was a church on every other corner (of course, the bars were as plentiful as the churches; one or the other could be found on every corner, but the bars were busier). Just up from the train depot along the Lincoln Highway, St. Joe's sat on one end of the street, with First Presbyterian just a couple blocks away. My mom was Catholic, Dad was Presbyterian, so we had the pick of the two. It wasn't a hard choice to make. My dad wasn't home much on Sunday, since he was usually working as an engineer with the Pennsylvania Railroad. And since Mom was the parent taking us to church, we went to St. Joe's.

On the inside, St. Joe's was (and still is) beautiful, with its stainedglass windows, high ceilings, and beautiful arches. We went there for mass on Sundays and throughout the week for school. The building seemed even bigger and more beautiful when I was in fifth grade. I remember good times at school.

One day my friend John DiPietro was sitting next to Ronnie Ball in church. Ronnie wasn't a Catholic; he went to public school, but that day he had off, so he came with us to mass. Confessional booths lined either side of the sanctuary, open for the spiritual business of students. In the middle of the mass, Ronnie turned to John and said, "I gotta go to the bathroom. Where are they?"

Without a blink, John said, "They're right over there," pointing to the wooden structure with the maroon drapery over the door. Ronnie got up, walked over to the booth, and went inside. You could hear him fumbling around inside. Finally he peeked out with a funny look on his face, then went back in. John and the boys with him in the pew all began giggling. On the other side of the screen, Father Fralick soon figured out what was up. "Son," he said, "who told you to come in here?" Then, louder; "Would *somebody* come get this child out of here?" Ronnie exited the booth, and before he took off for the bathroom, his smoldering eyes turned on John with the wordless threat *Just wait till church is over!*

A big altar at the front of the sanctuary held a wonderful crucifix. I still touch it when I visit there. I was an altar boy, helping the priest into his vestments in a little room on the side of the altar, helping with the candles, carrying the Bible. Sometimes I would sing. And whenever that happened, Dad always made sure he was in town for it.

When Dad was home on Sunday, we would walk down the street a little way from St. Joe's for the movie matinee at The Crest. In the first week of April 1956, The Crest was playing *The Phantom from 10,000 Leagues* along with *The Day the World Ended*, an ominous double feature.

For other recreation, Crestline offered a bowling alley with lanes, billiards, and a snack bar. My dad frequented the establishment. It offered dozens of leagues to join, so a person could bowl nearly every night of the week. Some people did.

Playing games was a big deal in Crestline. Maybe it's because the men worked so hard on the trains and the women worked so hard at home, but nearly everybody played games of some sort. On Sunday evenings, twenty or more people would gather in our little house to play canasta. The men and boys eventually tired of cards and went outside for sports.

Crestline was a big sports town. Every kid grew up around sports, and every father in Crestline wanted his boy to play ball. They talked about it everywhere.

Our little town supported as many as twenty-five bars, and in every bar, sports was the conversation. Paul, who still lives there, owned a bar called Andy's, on the South Side. He'll tell you that arguments broke out all the time about sports scores and records and rules. To settle fights, Paul kept record and rule books behind the counter. Whenever a couple of guys started a heated discussion about scores or records or rules, Paul told them to place their bets on the argument—five dollars—in an envelope, then Paul would seal it up and put it under the counter. Then he'd check the books, find out the answer, read it out loud, and give the envelope to the winner. This procedure avoided a ton of brawls.

■

In addition to bars and churches, trains and games, Crestline was blessed with two huge junkyards. A different Moyer brother owned each. Shorty Moyer ran the yard on the South Side, while Toad Moyer owned the westside business. With cars stacked four or five high and parts and other junk stretched over acre upon acre, they attracted customers from all over the Midwest.

For a cold pop, some of us kids would work for them. They paid us ten cents to find steel in the yards. We'd bring it back and Toad or Shorty would weigh it out and give each of us a dime to buy a pop from the machine. None of us were allergic to work, and we learned early that good things can come from working hard. And working hard *together*, as a town or a team or a family, was even better.

We lived just a little way from the South Side junkyard. My cousins, the Harbaughs—Judy, Janet, Jerry, Jack, and Jim— lived close by. Down the street, Gabe Hoke, an old black man, normally sat outside in a lawn chair on his porch, waving to everybody. Next to the Hokes lived the DiPietros, Jo-Jo and Johnny. We were all good friends. If we could have, we'd have spent every waking moment playing together.

All of us kids met up each morning as we walked along the street—the Gottfrieds, the Harbaughs, the DiPietros, along with a bunch of other kids, merging and streaming on our way to Catholic school. Some of them would wait for us in the swings across the street from our house. We'd all go down the street together, cross the tracks, and head for school.

Grandma Fisher lived at the end of our block. Often I would come up the street toward Grandma's on my way to school and sneak in for a treat—she made *the best* sugar cookies. My mother's aunt, Aunt Emmie, lived down the block on the other side of our house. Families stayed close to each other in those days.

After school, we'd get together and play ball. We had no trouble finding a spot because no one had fences. One yard just spilled into the next, through the whole block. Our backyards were like parks—and great places to play ball.

We were always hitting baseballs into Mr. Hart's yard. It didn't seem to matter where we played, we'd manage to hit them in there. His yard was like a baseball magnet. He lived on the corner and had the best-looking lawn on the South Side. You never wanted to hit a ball into the Hart yard because you never knew if he was home or not—and you never dared to go onto his lawn to get a stray ball. When he wasn't around, his lawn could be covered with baseballs. And when he arrived home, he'd gather them all up and take them into his garage. What he did with them, I'll never know.

While Mr. Hart could be grumpy about stray baseballs, everybody else in our neighborhood was friendly and kind. Right behind our house sat a small church, attended by black families who lived on the South Side. We kids never thought much about race. I suppose the adults talked about it, but if bad things were said, we didn't hear it, and if bad things were done, we didn't know about it. Some of my good neighborhood friends were black, and it didn't make any difference to me what color skin they had. All of us were friends with everybody else.

Relationships between blacks and whites were casual and friendly. We took care of each other. The black kids played with us and we played with them. We played sports together and we went to school together.

In only one place in town did race seem to matter much. At the swimming pool, blacks could swim on only one day, Tuesday, the day before the pool was cleaned. When we were swimming, black kids stood outside, looking in and waiting for Tuesday. I was often outside with them, holding on to the fence. It would be hot and my good friend Gates Brown would lean his head against that chain-link fence; he'd have grid marks on his face when he looked up. Gates used to say to me, "Mike, you gotta get in there and swim." But I told him, "I'm okay right here with you." I liked standing there with him, and something inside me felt bothered that we couldn't swim together.

Other than the business of the pool, I remember a kind of color blindness in Crestline. Everybody just seemed to get along. I'm sure that in a different town or in a bigger city, people acted differently. But I grew up not knowing what a racial slur was. I don't recall a single time I ever heard such a thing. Everybody spent time with each other and enjoyed each other, adults and kids alike, and they treated each other with respect.

Years later, respect and color blindness would come back to serve me well—yet another lesson God taught me in Crestline.

That's not to say that everyone in Crestline was perfect, of course! We had our little troublemakers.

Ray Scheiber ran a small store, no bigger than a living room, a couple of doors down from my house. We could go in there and say, "I'm gonna charge a candy bar," and from his wheelchair he'd get out a tablet and write down five cents. You couldn't charge a lot, but your mom would send you down to Scheiber's store to get milk and a loaf of bread, staples and treats. Sometimes the kids would say, "Mr. Scheiber, we want to get some salt," or something like that—anything just so he'd turn around with his back to them—and then they'd grab something off the counter, maybe a piece of candy or gum. I always wondered if Mr. Scheiber knew all along that they were grabbing things. I think he probably figured out exactly what they were doing and just added it to their bill.

Those were the days when we could leave empty glass milk bottles out at night on the front porch and the milkman would come by early in the morning to give us new ones. Everybody left the money for the milk out there, too. One morning the neighbors called my mother to tell her that their milk money had vanished. They had seen my brother Joe and his cousin Judy going around to every porch and collecting the cash. The milk money on the porches had proved too much of a temptation, and Joe and Judy were too young to understand what they'd done. But they never did it again!

Sometimes we played "ditch" in the public schoolyard across the street from our house. My cousin Jerry Harbaugh would climb out on the ledges under the third-story windows of the schoolhouse, about twenty-five feet up. The ledges provided a space not more than two or three inches wide, but he'd climb out there to play ditch. We were supposed to get him and tap him out. But nobody other than Jerry wanted to climb out on those ledges. If he ever fell, he could have killed himself. But as it was, he won the game every time.

■

While not everything in Crestline was perfect, my family came pretty close. Just as he did with Crestline, God put me into my family on purpose, according to his plans. The Gottfried family is where I belonged.

My early memories of my family center on one house, located on the other side of the street from the public school and next to an empty lot. Scheiber's store sat next to the lot. In the early spring, the lot would fill with dandelions, covering the ground with yellow. I loved that! I'd always say, "We have flowers!" And Mom would say, "No, you don't want those flowers. Those are weeds!" But it was beautiful.

So was my mom. Her name was Julia, but everybody called her Curly because of her brown, curly hair. In my mind I can still see her standing by the dandelions, the flowers drawing attention to her own simple beauty. She worked hard washing the clothes and hanging them on the line in the low field behind the house. She was always working, cooking and cleaning for us. Mom stayed home while Dad worked the trains, and he was usually gone for two or three days at a stretch. It was normal back then for a mom to stay at home.

We had a small house. The front room blended into the kitchen down a little hall. We had two bedrooms upstairs, and all of us kids slept in the same room and in the same bed: Joe was four years older than I, Johnny was four years younger, and all of us slept in the same bed. Our parents had the other bedroom.

Johnny was a firecracker. Of all of us, he acted the most like Dad; at least, that's what Grandma always said. He liked to tag along wherever the rest of us were going. Sometimes Mom wouldn't let him come along, but most of the time he was around.

My brother Joe was the best. He was a great ballplayer and a good student. He loved sports of all kinds and played any chance he got. He kept box scores with Dad when they listened to games on the radio. Joe and I would take baseball cards and spread them across the living room floor, organizing the teams and putting them in games, moving the cards around the carpet as if we were the coach or manager. Joe wanted to be a coach someday. A lot of kids in town wanted to be a coach—including me.

From the time I was able to play, I wanted to be a coach. My dad had always dreamed of being a coach, but he took a job on the trains instead so he could earn a good living and support his family. Working on the railroad appealed to me, but more than anything, I wanted to be a coach. When I grew up, I just knew I was going to coach football.

On the side of our house Dad made a basketball court, the hoop mounted on the garage. We played football in the low yard behind the house, or we played baseball anywhere we could. There was *always* some game going on. And Dad was always a part of it when he was home.

If we played against the other teams from the East Side or North Side, we met at Kelly Park, the other park in town. Kelly Park attracted teams and kids and adults from all corners.

Coach Hutson ran a little concession next to the pool where you could get a pop or some candy.

A little spit of a stream crossed under a footbridge in a gully that ran into the park. Because Crestline was a railroad town, the stream always had a slimy covering of diesel oil and tar and other unknown substances. We called it Stink Crick because it smelled like gasoline. Today it would be a cleanup site. When someone hit a grounder to right field and the ball rolled toward Stink Crick, we'd all be yelling, "Get the ball! Get it quick!" Once the ball got into Stink Crick, it never played the same; it would weigh a lot more and smell like tar. And pity the poor kid who had to go into the crick after the baseball!

Remember my friend Gates Brown, who used to encourage me to go swimming? We never worried about him hitting a ball into the crick. Even when he was eight or nine, he could hit the ball higher and farther than anybody else. He'd rear back, bend his knees, and let the bat fly, and the ball would go over the trees around the perimeter of the park and into somebody's yard. He played for the Big South Siders, and one day he would play for the Detroit Tigers, helping them win the 1968 World Series. Twice he led the American League in pinch hits.

We played until dark, until we could hardly see the ball, until one of us heard our mom calling us to come home.

The South Siders never wanted to quit; we never wanted to stop playing. It would be time for dinner, the sun almost gone. We'd barely be able to see and we knew it was time to head home. I can still hear my mom—when we wouldn't stop and go home—her voice calling out all over the South Side like a song: "*Jo*-oe! *Mi*-ike! *John*-ny!" And we'd be up in the park playing kick-the-can or baseball or something, dragging it on and on and on. I was the worst.

The other kids would say, "We gotta stop and go home."

And I'd say, "No! Let's keep playing."

"But I heard your mom. She's calling for you to come home." They would gather their gloves and bats and turn to go. I'd hold on to the ball, ready for the next pitch.

"C'mon, guys! Let's keep going. Who's up to bat?"

I just never wanted to stop playing. I never wanted to quit. I wanted to stay out at the park or on the field as long as I could. I wanted to stretch each day, each game. I wanted the game to go on *forever*.

That's the way with kids, and that is the way with life. We think it should last forever.

Of course, it doesn't.

FILL THE GAP

While I had a pretty idyllic childhood, unfortunately, not everyone does. A lot of boys grow up without any dad at all. They have no memory of a father, no recollection of a positive male role model.

So what tends to happen to such boys?

I've been in sports my whole life, so I know how to use numbers and manipulate statistics to "prove" just about anything. Still, some statistics just slap you in the face; there's no arguing with them. I think the following statistics fit into that category.

Remember that the following numbers don't necessarily identify causes, and they certainly don't imply that a boy without a functional father is doomed. If that were the case, I would have wound up with a dismal life. But each of these stats should make all of us sit up and take notice.

> • Eighty percent of the children who were "postwar generation" could expect to grow up with two biological parents married to each other. Today, only about 50 percent of our children will spend their entire childhood in an intact family. About 24 million children in America sleep in homes where their natural father does not live.[1]

---

1.   *Alabama Department of Human Resources.*

• Nationally, 40 percent of children whose fathers live outside the home have no contact with them. The other 60 percent had contact an average of sixty-nine days during the year. More than a quarter of absent fathers live in a state other than where their children reside.[2]

• Children from father-absent homes are five times more likely to live in poverty, three times more likely to fail in school, two to three times more likely to develop emotional and behavioral problems, and three times more likely to commit suicide.[3]

• The chief predictor of crime in a neighborhood is the percentage of homes without fathers. Up to 70 percent of adolescents charged with murder are from fatherless homes. Up to 70 percent of long-term prison inmates grew up in fatherless homes.[4]

• Children with involved, loving fathers are significantly more likely to do well in school, have healthy self-esteem, exhibit empathy and pro-social behavior, and avoid high-risk behaviors such as drug use, truancy, and criminal activity compared to children who have uninvolved fathers.[5]

---

2. Alabama Department of Human Resources.
3. Ibid.
4. Ibid.
5. National Fatherhood Initiative.

- Even after controlling for family background variables such as the mother's education level, race, family income, and number of siblings, as well as neighborhood variables such as unemployment rates and median income, boys who grew up outside of intact marriages were, on average, more than twice as likely as other boys to end up in jail.[6]

- 63 percent of youth suicides occur in fatherless homes.[7]

- 85 percent of all children who exhibit behavioral disorders come from fatherless homes.[8]

- 80 percent of rapists motivated by displaced anger come from fatherless homes.[9]

- 71 percent of all high school dropouts come from fatherless homes.[10]

- 70 percent of juveniles in state-operated institutions come from fatherless homes.[11]

- 85 percent of all youths sitting in prisons grew up in a fatherless home.[12]

---

6. National Fatherhood Initiative.
7. U.S. DHHS, Bureau of the Census.
8. Centers for Disease Control.
9. *Criminal Justice and Behavior* 14, p. 403–26.
10. National Principals Association report on the state of high schools.
11. U.S. Department of Justice, special report, September 1988.
12. Fulton County, Georgia, jail populations and Texas Department of Corrections, 1992.

Nobody can replace a father in a boy's life, but no boy needs to grow up without a positive male role model. As you continue to read this book, start asking yourself, "What fatherless boys do I know? And how could I make a difference in the life of at least one of them?"

CHAPTER TWO

A DAD TO REMEMBER

Dads are appointed by God to fill a place in the hearts of their kids. Dads aren't God, of course; every son or daughter learns that soon enough! But the place a dad fills is not mom-shaped—she has a place of her own. But a distinctive and predetermined place in the family portrait of every child ever born is saved specifically for dad.

In my family, that place was filled by Frederick Gottfried—"Fritz" to his friends, which was pretty much everybody in town. To us, he was just Dad. No other person in my life has been able to match the impact he made on me. Dad's place in my heart is his alone, and that's the way God planned it.

My father was not perfect, but he offered to all of us his love and his joy. And when he was gone, he left a big hole.

Dad was a railroad man, an engineer, and he loved people and sports, mostly in that order. For his entire short life, he always wanted to be a coach. He attended Findlay College for one semester, then, to provide for his family, he left school and got a job on the railroad. He never fulfilled his dream of being a coach—at least, not officially.

All his life he was involved in athletics in one way or another. He was a coach in many ways, all of them important and none of them official. He was our family coach. He taught us how to play—baseball, basketball, football, bowling—whatever happened to be the sport of the season. He helped and encouraged us, as a coach needs to do. And he didn't limit it just to us; anybody in our yard, at the park, or playing two-on-two in the living room of our little house had a coach named Fritz.

Dad invited over other kids to play nearly as much as we invited them. He loved all the kids in the community, and they all loved him. Adults liked him, too, all over town. Everywhere we'd go, people seemed happy to see him. He was friendly, gentle, and generous. And wherever he went, a group of boys always followed. He may have lacked the official title, but most definitely he was a coach.

It was my dad who organized the first ever Crestline Booster Club, and it was Dad who started the town's Little Leagues. He thought there ought to be an organized way for the kids to play baseball. So he and a couple other dads put the program together and worked on the field, the backstop, and the fencing. So many of us played every day, in the park or in a field or in the street, that we were becoming a mob in need of structure.

Dad wanted to make it easier for us to play, and he knew that organization would enable us to do it right and learn better from the experience. Dad willingly let us play in the house, have friends over and start the league, all because he wanted his boys to have something he never had.

He was a coach at heart.

Dad not only enjoyed the coaching role, he loved to play himself—basketball, football, shooting pool—anything. Watching was also good; he'd organize games just for the joy of looking on. He avidly listened to sports on the radio. He'd find a game on the airwaves and listen intently in the living room, with a score chart in front of him the whole time. Dad relished the chance to chart *any* game, and he taught Joe how to keep up the scores. At the beginning of a broadcast game, the three of us boys would sit on the floor of our living room around the radio, just as you see in pictures, and Dad would be bent over toward the speaker, listening and making notes on his charts.

It didn't take long for me to get bored—I was antsy—and I'd be off to shoot baskets or swing or play hide-and-seek. Johnny was too young to listen for long, so he'd get up and play. But Joe had patience and would sit there with Dad for the whole game.

They'd listen mostly to Ashland games and Mansfield High School games on station WMAN, but Dad rolled the dial until he found any game; it didn't really matter where it was or who was playing, high school or college or the Indians. When we got one of the first TVs in town, we'd sit around and watch sports on it; but there weren't a lot of games on TV, and we had poor reception. We'd have to constantly fiddle with the rabbit ears to get even a grainy picture. Dad preferred the radio, but thought live sports were better still.

Watching any of us play thrilled him, but he especially liked going to Joe's high school games. Joe would run home after playing ball, in a hurry to talk to Dad about the game. They'd discuss what went well and what didn't, what worked and what didn't.

Dad always said, "I can't *wait* to see you guys play." In the future that my father had in mind, each of us would excel in high school sports, go on to play college ball, and maybe even further. For a man who appreciated sports and wanted to be a part of things, Fritz Gottfried settled in the right town. Athletics was a part of us, woven into the fabric of our immediate family, of our neighborhood, of our whole town.

And Dad made sure of it.

∎

The basketball court outside our house attracted a crowd during the spring, summer, and fall. Even when it snowed, Dad would shovel off the court so we could play. But every year around the same time, in the bitter winter, the cold and snow of north-central Ohio would finally win out and run us inside. Crestline lies in the snowbelt of the upper Midwest, and we always had plenty of the white stuff. By November, the accumulation of snow usually closed the court by the garage.

Dad, however, came to the rescue.

My father put up a basketball court *inside* our house, right in the middle of our small living room. First he made a hoop out of a wire clothes hanger bent into a loop and hung over a door on one end of the room. In a hallway on the other side he taped the other hoop up on the wall. We had a little ball that just fit the hoops. Dad would move all the furniture out of the way—chairs, couch, everything. We had no new belongings, so it was okay to move the stuff around. At least, it was okay with Dad.

Not so much with Mom! I can remember her saying—most of the time with a smile on her face—"You're not gonna move those things *again*!" And Dad would move everything anyway. She'd say, "*What* are you guys doing?" but he'd organize the teams. She'd say, "You're going to *ruin* this house," but in no time at all we'd be playing two-on-two and he'd be on one of the teams, my brothers and I making up the other players.

Mom's protests became part of the game.

Sometimes Johnny, about seven at the time, would sit and watch because he could get trampled on that tiny court. Dad would team up with me. Joe, around fifteen, would play with my cousin Jack. The four of us would push around that living room as if it were a gymnasium or a stadium. We'd pass that little ball and defend when we needed to, just as if we were in the big leagues, just like Buckeyes. When Joe persisted in throwing his size around, defending the basket, Dad would hold him back and let me dunk one on him.

Some days our little living room would be crammed with

maybe nine boys—twelve, counting us three. We could play only two-on-two in there, but the other kids would come over and watch, sitting on the couch and the floor to wait their turn. If my dad was home, he'd be coaching, playing, and replacing the hoops when they fell off.

It could get pretty physical; that's what Mom really didn't like. Once when we were playing a big game, one of my cousins went crashing through the window. He was okay, but the accident slowed down the living-room basketball games for a while. After a few days, though, Dad was back organizing teams for another game. That's just the way he was.

When Dad was out of town on a railroad trip, Mom wouldn't put up with the living-room basketball. All games were "called due to Mom." We were not allowed to move the furniture around, not allowed to throw the ball in the house, and not allowed to put up the hoops.

Until Dad got home again!

In the hallway from the living room to the kitchen, Dad found a place to hang a swing. This red swing ran straight through the middle of our house. He pounded that thing into the doorframe and mounted it there for my brothers and me. We'd sit in the swing and push back into the living room and let it fly, our feet stretching into the kitchen. Mom would be cooking supper and somebody would swing by, his feet close to hitting her, so close she had to dodge.

Swinging away, back and forth from kitchen to living room,

I remember going by the oven close to mom and coming out the other way. She'd say, "What are you doing?" as if she didn't see exactly what I was doing. I'd say, "I'm just swing-ing," as if I had to tell her. Then Dad would say, "Let him swing." And she did.

Mom understood and let Dad have his fun. He worked hard for the railroad, and when he wasn't working hard there, he was working hard to make time for his kids. That red swing stood for something: it stood for my dad's willingness to push a few rules and bend a few conventions so that his boys could enjoy life and so that he could enjoy us. He was swinging right along with us, even though he couldn't sit in that red swing himself. Our fun was his fun, and he just wanted to make the house a place where his kids could do enjoyable things.

In these ways and many more, Dad gave us *attention*. He has served as a model for my own life when it comes to this im-portant father-function. When I've been forced to be on the road over the years, I've tried to make sure that I spent my days at home with my girls. I've tried to live up to my father's exam-ple of helping my children know I am attentive to their needs— not just for food, clothing, and "stuff," but their need for my time and attention.

Dad liked his job on the trains. But the railroad job meant he'd be gone for two or three days at a time, usually making a run between Conway and Pitcairn, Pennsylvania. He worked what they called the action board; the odd shifts and odd hours allowed him to make more money. His frequent absence made things hard on my mom, but when he'd get back in town, we always had a celebration.

It felt great to hear Mom say, "Hey, Dad's coming home tomorrow!" Mom would find out when Dad would be getting back, then she'd drive us out to County Line Road along the tracks so we could all get out of the car and wave at Dad as he came by. He would wave back from the train and we'd shout and call to him. Then we'd go down to the yard to pick him up.

The yard was a huge roundhouse featuring thirty stalls with a hundred-degree turntable. The engineers had a locker room, and we'd impatiently wait for Dad to come out. Sometimes he'd put us on the train and let us ride it into the yard. We always felt a little sad when he had to leave, but we always had a celebration when he came home. It excited all of us.

When he was in town, he invested time in his kids. He always centered his time at home on us. Dad's schedule didn't allow him to get too involved at church, but since I was an altar boy, he would come whenever he could. One night around Christmas I sang a solo at church, "O Holy Night." The family made a big deal out of it and Dad made sure he was there to hear me.

When Dad had finished a trip, he'd come home tired, having worked all night long. But he never felt so tired that he wouldn't spend time with his boys. He wanted to know all about what we were doing in school, what was happening in the neighborhood, and mostly how our games were going. Part of being a good dad is this sacrificial accommodation, the kind of thing my father was especially good at. It meant pushing his own agenda aside and making room in his life for his children.

I can remember him coming home, exhausted from working all night, and he'd try to get one or two of us to come lie down with him and talk to him until he fell asleep. We'd all pile on the bed and he'd close his eyes, ask us about our days, listen as we told him what game we had played and the final scores, and how the Indians were doing. Before long we'd look up and see that he'd drifted off to sleep.

Dad loved to get away on vacations. They could never be for long, since he had to be at work, but he made sure we got away once in a while.

He'd pack up the car with kids, filling every available seat and all the spaces in between with as many boys and girls as possible. The Harbaughs never went on vacation, so we always had a couple of cousins with us. Then Dad would swing by other homes on his way out of town, so long as he still had any room left in the car. He'd pull up into a driveway and yell, "Anybody want to go to Charleston?"

We went to Charleston, West Virginia, to visit relatives. Our favorite was Uncle Jack, a big, fun guy. But the main attraction was that Uncle Jack used to play baseball. When we visited Uncle Jack, we always went to a baseball game with a minor-league team called the Charleston Senators. Uncle Jack would take us down to his basement and show us his bats—

real, genuine big-league baseball bats. I couldn't even lift them, they were so heavy; but I dreamed of the day I could. And Dad seemed just as interested in Jack's stories (and his bats) as we were.

Fritz Gottfried loved his boys, and everybody in Crestline knew it. He didn't keep his love for us a secret. We could do no wrong in his eyes—but that's not to say that he overlooked it when we misbehaved.

Part of being a father is dishing out discipline when it is needed. Loving discipline gives children the advantage of *authority*. Having somebody in charge offers a child stability and safety, and Dad gave that gift to us. He never indulged us and he knew how to be tough when necessary. He expected us to be good, and we generally rose to his expectations. Dad didn't have to discipline us often—but when he did, it meant something.

I can remember my father having to discipline me only one time. It's not that he didn't do it more than once or that I was a perfect kid, it's just the only time I remember his doing it. I don't remember what I had done. Maybe it was lighting matches under the front porch with Jim? Whatever it was, I vividly remember Dad looking for me, and that I was in trouble. I tried to hide, hoping that I could outsmart him and get to a place where he couldn't find me. So I crawled under the dining table, hoping that somehow he'd forget about the infraction and I'd be off the hook.

I remember Dad reaching under the table, waving his arms to try to get a hold on whatever body part he could use to pull me out. His frustration mounted the more I kept squirming around, dodging his grip. Finally, in a quick and fateful move, he grabbed my ankle and pulled me out.

I don't remember what I did, but I am absolutely *sure* I never did it again.

Mom wanted us to go to Catholic school, so Dad made sure it happened. His work schedule prevented him from becoming actively involved in our school activities, but he talked about school all the time. He talked about the teachers, the nuns, and how we should respect them. He talked about how important school was and how we should do well. When we did well, he affirmed us, told us we were doing a great job, patted us on the back, and made us feel good.

Dad's *affirmation* helped us to know we had value and that we were important to him. By affirming, a father lets his kids know what he feels is important; at the same time, his kids appropriate his value system. We learned what Dad thought was important through his "affirmative actions."

In our home it was a given that the family supported the school and the school supported the family. Mom knew the Catholic school nuns were tough, but I still didn't want to tell her when I got in trouble, even though she was always understanding. Dad loved the nuns. Even as a Presbyterian, he appreciated the strict nature of a Catholic school education.

I tell you, those nuns scared me. When you'd go to school and they'd say, "Stand up and read that paragraph," you had better be reading that paragraph *right*! The nuns and the priest had my attention, and I knew Mom and Dad would back them up and not put up with any shenanigans. I didn't want to disappoint my parents or the nuns—but every now and then, I'd get into trouble.

Once in third grade I went to the chalkboard to do an arithmetic problem in front of the class. When I had some trouble with it, the sister got on me. I tried, but I just couldn't figure out the problem—and the passing of time had a distinct impact on my bladder. I finally dropped the chalk and had "an accident."

I sprinted out of the classroom at a full run and fled the school as fast as I could. I ran home and into my house, where Mom was in the kitchen. She looked me over and said, "What are you doing home?"

"I couldn't do this arithmetic problem at the chalkboard," I answered. She looked me up and down and quickly knew it was more than just an arithmetic issue.

"You're going to have to go back," she declared. She helped get me changed and then took me back to the school and directly to the nun. Mom apologized for my running out and asked if I could come back to class.

Dad heard about the whole episode when he came home, but he didn't punish me. He figured that I had been embarrassed enough by the whole thing and that he didn't need to add any more to it.

A good dad knows when enough is enough.

We often got in the car and went up to the lake, about an hour from us. We'd just sit by the water or go to the beach or fish.

Dad was a good fisherman and took us along whenever he could. Of course, we'd swing by the Harbaughs and the DiPietros and invite them to join us, along with anybody else who was standing around.

Crestline had a dam that pooled water from a stream. The dam had no name, such as the Hoover Dam or the Coolee Dam; we just called it "the dam." The railroad had built it to service the steam trains and the boilers.

The dam became our fishing hole. I had no patience for catching fish, so Dad always told me, "Now, Mike, you've got to be patient. You've got to sit down here and wait on these fish." As a rambunctious kid, I thought the fish should bite all the time. I'd get fidgety and want to swim or splash around, effectively scaring the fish off. I'd pull up on the pole, my bobber would go down, and I'd think I'd caught something really big. Dad would laugh and say, "Be patient, Mike."

Patience has always been a hard lesson for me. I'm not sure I have it down yet.

One night Dad took us out gigging for frogs. We stayed out all night, catching the frogs and putting them into a big bucket. The next morning, Dad handed me the big potato bag full of frogs to carry into the house. So many frogs filled the heavy bag that I dropped it, sending hopping frogs jumping away in every direction. We laughed ourselves silly as we scrambled and fumbled around on our hands and knees, trying to scoop up those frogs as fast as we could. Most of them escaped—and Dad just laughed. He knew we hadn't wasted a night just because the frogs got away. In fact, those wonderful memories live on today. (And those frogs may still be alive in Crestline somewhere.)

I loved fishing with my dad. He'd help us with the lines and bait our hooks for us. He'd talk and joke and we'd laugh. It was pure family at its best. There's *nothing* like going fishing with your dad. Nothing!

Those times with my father made me feel accepted, as if I belonged to someone, as if I fit into someone's plans. Smart fathers, like my dad, make sure their children know they are part of the family and part of him. He creates a team and welcomes his family as part of that team. He validates their purpose in life by helping them to know they are wanted and that they belong. He practices *acceptance*.

When I went fishing with my dad, I knew I was wanted in this world, that I belonged, that I was loved. And I wanted it to go on forever.

My dad always accepted me no matter what, but I do remember one time when I really felt his disappointment in me. I knew I had let him down.

As the spring approached, Dad had been working on the train for a couple days. He wanted the baseball field to be in top shape for the upcoming Little League season, and so he asked Mr. Oswalt to pick up my younger brother and me and work on the field. Mr. Oswalt came by along with his son, Ricky, who played on our team, and he brought the three of us to the field to help him bring it up to Crestline Little League standards.

Instead, we started playing games and got to playing hide-and-seek. The other two boys—Johnny, who was five, and Ricky—ran into a little utility shed near the ball field to hide. I was "it" and was poking around outside the shed, trying to find them. I had an idea that they might be hiding inside, so I peeked into the gaps of the wooden slats on the shed.

Ricky picked up a board and started throwing it around to scare me, while Johnny tried to hide in the corners. In the darkness, Ricky threw the board toward the place I was standing outside. At that moment, Johnny came out of hiding and moved directly in front of the board. It caught Johnny square in the face, stabbing into his eye.

Johnny came screaming out of the shed, stumbling and holding his eye, blood dribbling through his hands. Ricky and I panicked, but Mr. Oswalt took things into control, hurriedly got us all back in the car, and raced Johnny to the hospital.

Mom came as soon as she got the call, and Dad hurried home as soon as he learned what had happened. The doctors were doing everything they could, but it was a serious injury. Johnny stayed in the Crestline hospital for three days, then got transferred to Mansfield General, in a bigger city to our east. Mom and Dad drove all of us there. Johnny remained at Mansfield General for three weeks. The whole time, doctors attempted to do everything they could to save Johnny's eye.

Later, they sent Johnny to the Cleveland Clinic, but no one could do anything. Mom almost broke down because of it, feeling helpless and discouraged. Dad kept his quiet composure.

Johnny eventually lost his eye.

On the day of the accident, I didn't know what to expect when my dad came home. I hadn't thrown the board, but I should have been working. I felt a big load of guilt. Dad sat in our living room with me and said, "My God, how could this happen?"

I knew he was upset. He told me he was angry about what had happened, but he knew no one was to blame. He felt disappointed that we had been goofing around instead of helping. But he put his arm around me anyway and I knew I was forgiven.

When my dad showed me *affection* during that difficult time, he used one of the most powerful tools a father has to help his children know they are unconditionally loved. When a dad puts his arm around his kid, gives him a hug or a kiss, pats her back or touches her face, he speaks volumes of love that mere words cannot communicate.

Dad created the safest place on earth for me when he placed his arm around my shoulder. And he did it even when he felt disappointed in me, even when I felt miserable and unlovable.

Dad never said it, but I believe Johnny's accident made him upset with himself. I believe he felt far more guilty than anyone else did. He felt he should have been there, that if he had been in town, things might have turned out differently.

In late winter of 1956, Dad got a job offer that would take us to Buffalo, New York. It was a great job. He didn't want to move his family, but it would mean more income and a stable life with better hours. Expenses were mounting because of Johnny's accident the previous spring, so the increased salary would help. Dad would be home more, since he wouldn't have to ride all the time. Above all, he wanted to do the right thing by his wife and children. He loved us.

We kids had a different perspective. None of *us* thought much of the idea. We loved Crestline and never wanted to leave. We didn't want anything to change. Why mess with a life you love?

Fortunately, the railroad didn't expect a decision until May, so we had plenty of time to think about the move. At least, that's what the calendar said.

A few months later, on the night of April 2, Dad and Joe went to the bowling alley to play some pool. Dad was winning—out way ahead. Joe got angry, missed a shot, and quit before the game ended.

Dad didn't like that a bit. He intended to teach us to follow through, no matter what, to never give up. "Joe," he told my brother, "never be a quitter." To this day, Joe remembers that lesson. In his successful career as a coach and athletic director, Joe has proved that he hasn't forgotten and has often reminded his players of the value of determination. That's the lesson Dad taught Joe that night—the last one he'd ever give.

After Dad and Joe returned home, Dad asked me to go back with him to the bowling alley. He liked one of us to go with him when he bowled; it was another way to spend time with each boy. He tried taking all of his sons, but I was the only one available that night. I had fun watching him bowl, and more fun listening to the talk and chatter of his team.

When we got back, he and I sat on the living-room couch. Mom made some popcorn and we shared a bowl and drank some pop. We talked and Dad asked me to make a promise, one I've never forgotten.

"I want you to promise me you're gonna be a good player," he said, "and I want you to promise me you'll be better than Joe."

Does that sound mean, as if he were pitting us against each other? But that's not what he was doing at all. Had he lived, he would have sat my younger brother down at some point and said to him, "Johnny, I want you to promise me you'll be a better player than Joe or Mike." Dad didn't do this to fuel competition between us, or to get back at Joe about his quitting fit earlier that evening. Dad used it to challenge me. Each of us already looked up to the next older one; we wanted to be just like him. Dad wanted to nurture that desire. So he asked me to promise to surpass Joe's example, an example he knew to be good.

I promised. I'm not sure I've been able to fulfill it, but I promised.

Sometime that night—in the early darkness before dawn on April 3, 1956—I heard Dad talking to Mom. By that hour, 3:30 a.m., I was usually asleep, but for some reason I didn't sleep at all that night. I could hear them talking in the next room.

"I'm not feeling good," my dad said. "I'm gonna get up."

"Okay, dear," Mom said.

I heard him get up, walk around his bed, and pad down the short hall to the bathroom. And then I heard a loud thump— and I wasn't the only one who heard it.

I went running down the hall to identify the loud noise, and Johnny came running after me; so did Joe. Mother was already in the bathroom and immediately took charge. I saw Dad laid out on the bathroom floor.

"Joe, go get the doctor." The doctor lived five doors down from us. Joe threw on his clothes, hurtled down the stairs, and ran down the street to the doc's house.

"Mike, put this washcloth on his head." She handed it to me. "Get it wet and put it on his forehead and help hold his head up."

She ran out of the room to get some things that she thought would help, though I don't know what they could have been. I sat there on the bathroom floor. Dad was lying on his back, his head in my lap. He was moaning, no words, just moaning and groaning. His lips had begun turning blue.

Johnny stood in the hallway door. I still have that picture in my mind of my little brother as he watched me and stared at my father on the floor.

I began talking to Dad. "Joe's going for the doctor, Dad. Mom's gone to get something to help. It's okay." I was so scared. I just did what Mom told me to do. I held the washcloth on his forehead, I don't know for how long. Not long, I know, but it seemed like forever. My heart pounded and I wanted to jump up and do *something* to help Dad. But I could do nothing except hold his head in my lap and pray. I felt completely helpless. I prayed hard.

At some point Joe returned, running up the stairs with the doctor, who immediately recognized the symptoms of a massive heart attack. My dad may have died in my arms, or it may have been a few minutes later.

But the next time I saw my father, he was in a casket.

I thought the good life we had in Crestline would go on and on and on. But everything I knew when I was eleven years old—about me, my family, my life—died with my dad that night.

None of us dreamed that we would go to bed that evening and, before the sun rose, see everything in our lives turned upside down. Dad had just been through a physical examination six months before. He appeared to be in great shape. The whole thing was incomprehensible to us.

And yet there it was on the front page of the April 5, 1956, *Crestline Advocate*:

Frederick Gottfried, 41, died suddenly Tuesday at 5:00 a.m. at his home, 514 N. Thoman St., shortly after arising to go to work. Death was attributed to coronary thrombosis.

Mr. Gottfried was born Dec. 9, 1914 at Upper Sandusky, the son of John F. and Jessie Yochum Gottfried. He was united in marriage with Julia Fisher of Crestline June 27, 1938, at Crestline. He came to Crestline 20 years ago and for the past 16 years has been employed by the Pennsylvania Railroad Company, and at the time of his death was an engineer for the company.

Survivors include his wife, Julia, and three children, Joe, Michael, and John, and his mother.

Funeral services will be held Friday at 1:30 p.m. at the Garverick Funeral Home. Internment will be in St. Joseph's Cemetery, Crestline. Friends may call at the funeral home starting Wednesday evening until time of service.

It was all a blur to me. I have only one clear memory of that day: holding my father's head in my hands as he died on the floor of the bathroom. I don't remember anything else. I know Mom sent Johnny and me to Grandma Fisher's house down the street early in the morning, but I don't even remember going.

I just didn't understand what had happened. It didn't sink in. A foggy gap arose between what I had seen and done and the truth about death. It would take some time before reality sank in.

When a crisis occurs, it's sometimes like the big roundhouse in the Crestline rail yard: turn in almost any direction and you'll find a track to take. But not all of those tracks lead to good places that God knows will bless you and form part of his good plan for your life.

When crisis struck my family, I got thrown into that roundhouse. I didn't know which way to go. I couldn't even tell you which way was up or down, left or right, north or south. At the time, I couldn't handle the truth. I was spinning in the roundhouse, dizzy with the sudden and tragic change in the direction of my young life.

Later that day, Joe went with Mom to the funeral home. Together, they made the necessary arrangements with Mr. Garverick, picking out a casket, deciding on the visitation, the service, the burial.

Dad was really dead. Gone. My life had shattered into a million pieces. There was still a family, there was still love, and there was still a God in heaven. In fact, God used the pain in my life to bring me face-to-face with my need for his guidance and help.

But there was no Dad anymore. The game was over, and I had a hole in my heart in the exact shape of my father.

FILL THE GAP

I sometimes look back on my life and wonder about the kind of man my dad was and why our dad was so great. Not everybody gets a great dad. God calls all fathers to be good dads, but not all of them live up to the call. My dad did. I think God wanted me to have a great dad so that when he was no longer around, I'd have a big hole in my heart.

That big hole has allowed me to understand profoundly what the emptiness of having no dad feels like. I needed to feel that emptiness so I could offer the right kind of help to boys who share the same hole in their hearts.

You probably noticed that as I described my dad, I emphasized five traits that made him into a great father. I believe that every good father provides these five things—call them father-functions. Every boy craves and needs each one. These functions form the outline of the gap an absent father leaves in a boy's heart.

In later chapters we'll take a closer look at each one, but for now, ponder the five father-functions that can make such a difference in the life of any boy.

1. Affection

A boy needs a man to pat him on the back, put a hand on his shoulder, give him a big hug and a kiss, give his backside a sports slap. That touch communicates *love beyond words*.

2. Attention

When my father put up a swing or mounted a basketball hoop or pushed some furniture out of the way for a game, he was going the extra mile to give us his attention. When he came home and spent time with us or invited us to the bowling alley or took us fishing, he demonstrated that he was willing to make sacrifices to *be around*. Did my father like playing ball and fishing? Sure. But that he truly wanted us along with him told us in clear, undeniable, wordless communication, "I think you're great and I like spending time with you."

3. Affirmation

Fathers convey worth to their children. They help their kids know they have value, that each child is placed on earth for some specific purpose and that each has a unique destiny. When Dad told me, "You did a good job, Mike," or, "That was a great play at first base," or "I liked the way you cleaned up for your mother," it plugged me into my family, my neighborhood, my team, my town, as a person who had something to offer. I became a *valuable person*.

4. Authority

Dad was in charge. What he said was the way it was. He never wielded his authority to hurt us or to anger us, but to help us and protect us. Proper authority from a father grounds a boy in confidence. The knowledge that someone higher, stronger, and smarter than me has my backside and is the *person in charge* allows me to function in a safer environment. That kind of loving leadership lays a solid foundation for taking risks and gives you the okay to be yourself.

5. Acceptance

Combine all of the above and what you have is a firm sense of belonging. My dad, through his actions and words, communicated to me that I was a part of something bigger, that I belonged to him. He didn't press this as "ownership," but he confirmed again and again—and never gave me any reason to doubt him—that I was *his* kid, *his* boy, a part of *his* family, along with Joe and Johnny. We were on a team, he was the coach, and we were in this thing together.

These are just a few of the things a dad gives his boys; there are others. But these are the ones I instinctively knew I had to replace once my dad was gone.

Every boy who loses his dad is looking, hunting, and scanning the landscape to find these five elements. He wants to share his successes. When he gets a good grade in school, he wants to tell someone about it. When he hits the ball well or rides his bike fast, he craves a word of congratulation from the person who knows him best and who loves him most. When he skins up a knee or gets in trouble, he longs for someone to offer help and healing. This sharing means more than almost anything.

In chapters to come I'll show what can happen when men choose to step into the gap created by the loss of a father. And I'll introduce you to some real-life kids whose lives *right now* are being enriched by generous men who choose to take up the challenge to fill the father gap.

CHAPTER THREE

A HOLE IN THE EXACT
SHAPE OF MY FATHER

The Gottfried family picture originally included my grand-mothers on both sides, my mother and father, Joe, Johnny, and me. But the morning my dad died, one prominent figure in the picture faded away, leaving behind a gaping, empty space in his exact shape.

I wish I could tell you that the picture was quickly restored by someone who fit exactly into that hole—but that just wouldn't be true. My mother remarried several years later, but her new husband didn't come close to filling that space. My older brother, Joe, tried to step into the extra responsibility almost as soon as Dad was gone, but he couldn't fill the gap, either. God certainly provided comfort and love during that time, but the empty space remained.

I believe that was on purpose.

The emptiness motivated me to begin a search for the things a father puts into a boy's life. At first I didn't even know I was looking. Only later did I realize I was on a hunt for someone or something to fill the empty hole.

Although everything was a blur during the three days of visitation, I remember looking at Dad's coffin and seeing its meaning with utter clarity. This was the end—and it was final.

At the cemetery when they lowered the coffin into the ground, it hit me again: *this is it.* Through a stream of tears, my eyes kept turning to look at the hole in the ground. As I stood there, a passing train blew its whistle. I cried harder.

The worst part of it was turning around and walking away. I didn't want to leave; I wanted to stay and talk to my dad. I wanted to be alone with him again, fishing or bowling or playing catch. I wanted to talk to him the way we did when he came home tired, up in his bed while he drifted off to sleep. It was all I could do to turn and walk away from the grave and out of the cemetery.

We went home, where lots of family and friends had gathered for a meal. Instead of the smell of food, the taste of death hung in the air and stuck to my tongue. I'm sure it was important for everyone to be around, but I wanted them to leave. I wanted to be alone. Later that day I walked back out to the cemetery, all by myself. I just sat on the ground, crying. Of course, another train soon came by—one of the loneliest sounds I'd ever heard.

A few weeks later Mom took all of us out to the cemetery to see Dad's grave marker. I could hardly look at it because it proved once again the finality of it all. It put yet another picture in my head that represented the awful truth: Dad was gone and he wasn't coming back.

While we stared at his gravestone, yet another Pennsylvania Railroad train whistle blew out a signal—but somehow, this one felt different. As I stood there with my remaining family, the sound did not feel quite so lonely and desolate as all the others. I took it as a sign, a good sign. It felt as if Dad wanted us to know *things are going to get better.*

Whenever I hear a train whistle today, I feel warmed by the goodness of God. It really does get better, even though healing may not happen right away.

■

The morning after the funeral, Mom sat us all down. She explained that we had no insurance money. The rent would be due in a few days, and she couldn't pay it. She would have to find another place for us to live. She would also need to find work, then take some time to get settled. That meant all of us boys would have to live with others for a while.

"I'll get us all back together as soon as I can," she promised. "I just have to take some time to figure out how we're going to do this." Mom was going to live with her aunt, Emma Miller. She had made arrangements for Joe and Johnny to live at Grandma Fisher's house. I went to the Harbaughs, our cousins. Mom had our bags packed and we walked out of the house on South Seltzer Street for good.

I felt glad to get out of there—the house just had too many sad memories. Besides, in just a little while we'd be back together again. And best of all, we were still in Crestline, where people cared and where God would start the healing.

The people around us made possible the first stages of our healing. It seemed as if the whole town of Crestline came to the Garverick Funeral Home for the three days of visitation. The funeral director said, "Your dad was a well-liked man. This will be one of the biggest funerals we've ever had." And it was.

The whole town seemed to be in shock. Since Fritz Gottfried was only forty-one years old, nobody had expected his death so soon or so quickly. Not one person failed to feel the powerful engine of grief and loss that had barreled down the tracks. Dad's death surprised us all.

Despite the shock, Crestline responded with compassion. Everyone in town chipped in. Food overflowed our house for days. People asked what they could do and inquired about Mom's circumstances and how they could help out.

A group of local men decided to start a fund. Coach Hutson and others from the school and the Little League put together a campaign to help pay for Johnny's eye surgeries. Jars placed all over town filled quickly. Volunteers gathered donations and put them into a special fund in the downtown bank. The *Advocate* reported on the campaign:

> *A move is underway to raise funds to take care of necessary medical work on the injured eye of Johnny Gottfried. Johnny's dad, Fritz Gottfried, passed away last week, and some of his friends thought it would be a good idea to preserve the memory of a great guy by helping his youngest son to see.*
>
> *The fund will be known as the Fritz Gottfried Memorial Fund. However, all the money will be used on Johnny's eye. The logic behind this move is simple. Fritz Gottfried was a wonderful man to know. His friends, even those of us who weren't lucky enough to know him for a very long time, were impressed by the love of sports that he held.*
>
> *Likewise, we were impressed to see the prodigious amounts of labor and time Fritz donated to watching, promoting, and participating in sports activities.*
>
> *We know that had he lived one of his greatest concerns would have been for the eye which Johnny injured last summer. It is with this in mind that the fund was originated.*
>
> *We know the fund will be a success. We congratulate the men who originated the idea and serve on the committee.*

The bowling leagues hosted a tournament to raise money for the fund. For weeks The *Advocate* maintained receipts and listed donors in every edition. Hundreds of individuals and businesses in Crestline contributed. Up and down the railroad line between Fort Wayne and Pittsburgh, people heard of the fund and gave out of fond remembrance of my father. The fund raised well over five thousand dollars, an amazing amount in those days—and a potent statement of Crestline's love for my dad.

The week after the funeral, Johnny, Joe, and I went back to school. Mom went out to find work. Life went on, whether we liked it or not. The Crestline Bulldog baseball team thrashed the Mansfield Tygers. Ronnie Ball bunted in a run and Joe Gottfried got a single in the fifth for another run, spearheading a 7–1 win. Dad would have been proud.

The surviving members of our family may have had to separate, but we still lived on the South Side—and the South Side took care of its own. I saw my brothers every day, went to school, and visited Mom. I wouldn't call my stay at the Harbaughs easy, but I made it through.

It took Mom more than three months to earn enough money to get us back together. We moved to Pearl Street, several blocks away, but now on the north side of town. Getting settled and back to some kind of normal routine gave us all some hope. Finally, we were a little more like a family. And it was a little more like home.

Our new place had a garage, so the day we moved in, we set up a basketball court. Before long, neighbor kids were coming over to play. The house had a small kitchen, a little front room, Mom's room, and my brothers and I shared a bedroom. Mom even let us put up a basketball hoop in the kitchen!

Every night I heard my mom crying in her room. Here she was, a single mom in a tiny town in the middle of Ohio, with three active boys to raise, all on her own. She did the best she could. She was thirty-six years old and a great mom. But I knew it was tough on her.

We felt blessed to have other relatives in Crestline: Mom's sister, Marie Harbaugh; and her brothers, Paul and Tom. They all contributed however they could and did their best to help manage things around our house. But all of them had families of their own—big families, and jobs that demanded lots of their time. Uncle Paul and Uncle Tom both worked the railroad, like my dad, so they had limited hours to give. Mom had to be both parent and provider almost entirely on her own.

Mom had never held a job outside the home before Dad's death. After the funeral, she hired on at Sherer's, a dairy farm that also operated a counter where truckers could come in to eat. Mom worked the counter as a waitress, mostly in the afternoons and evenings. She got good tips and the Sherers tried to do right by her. They let us have dinner with her during her shift—maybe a grilled-cheese sandwich, or some macaroni, or Sherer's famous hamburgers.

Mom worked hard. She wanted us to have everything and not think about what we'd lost. And in fact I never wanted for anything, even though today I know we were poor. I didn't know or even care what other people had. I had everything I needed. We ate well, wore decent clothes, and had a roof over our heads. We had the basic necessities of life, and that was enough.

But even so, as the emptiness settled in, the hole in my heart began to hurt in new ways.

It was especially tough for me at night. Because my mother worked the dinner shift, my brothers and I often came home to a parentless house. The absence of our father became sharply real to us and we felt a deep insecurity in the house. Dad was no longer there to watch over us, to be God's watchman over our home.

I often went to bed angry. I'd pray angry prayers, the way David does in some of the Psalms: "What the heck happened? Lord, why? Why did I have to lose my dad? Why now?" And I'd cry and cry some more. Every night I cried myself to sleep.

I also wet the bed. Joe got a bed to himself, while Johnny and I shared the other one. When I wet the bed—always around 3:00 a.m., close to when I'd heard Dad collapse on the morning he died—I'd say, "Johnny, get up and get in bed with Joe." But Johnny had to start every night with me.

While my insecurities revealed themselves in bed-wetting, they also served to push me into a new pursuit. From then on, I was on a search. I was looking for somebody to affirm me, somebody to spend some time with me, somebody to say, "Hey, you're doing a good job." I may not have been able to explain exactly what I was looking for, but I knew I was looking.

The dad-shaped hole in my family picture shouted out to be filled. Mom tried to do that for me, but it just wasn't the same. She provided affirmation, authority, and the rest, but she had no way to do it as only a father can.

Joe also did the best he could. He was mature enough to be a big help, but he was looking to fill the same hole in his own life. Joe describes it this way: "I just grabbed out for another man to take the place of Dad. I lost something and I was trying to put it back. I finally had to come to the place where I just stopped. Nobody could fill that place."

Joe visited the cemetery almost every day. "I wasn't ready to lose him," he remembers. None of us were ready to lose him, but we did the best we could to cope.

◼

A couple weeks after Dad's death, one of our cousins graduated from high school and we attended a party at her house. Joe sat in the living room, watching the festivities, and tears fell from his face. I knew what he was thinking: *Dad will never see me graduate from high school.*

I also remember when I learned to dribble the basketball; it was a big deal because I had the hardest time getting it down. I just couldn't catch the rhythm of it. But when it finally clicked, I thought, *This is pretty good!* I felt really excited.

But I came home that day to a house without a parent. And even if Mom *had* returned home from work, she wouldn't have known a dribble from a rebound. She just wouldn't have understood how important dribbling was to a guy. She'd congratulate me, but not from the standpoint of knowledge or experience.

A couple of months after my father died, the VFW hosted a father-son banquet. A front-page story in the *Advocate* announced the event:

> *Bob Feller, veteran pitcher for the Cleveland Indians, will be the featured speaker at a Father-Son Banquet to be given at the Veterans of Foreign Wars Hall, on June 18. Only a limited number of tickets will be sold. All interested fathers and sons are welcome to attend.*

Bob Feller was a hero to us, a great pitcher for the Cleveland Indians who eventually made it into the Hall of Fame. *Everyone* wanted to attend this event. I was supposed to attend with one of my uncles and his son. But the morning of the banquet, a fifth-grade classmate said to me, "I guess you can't go to the banquet tonight, huh?"

"What do you mean?" I asked. "Why not?"

"It's a father-son banquet," he replied, "and you don't have a father."

He didn't say it to hurt me. No malice was involved—but he said it, and it hurt anyway. It hurt big.

I didn't respond. I just got quiet. I went home and told my mom I wasn't going.

"Of course you're going," she said.

"I don't want to go," I insisted. "I don't have a dad."

"You're still going to go."

"No. Not going."

"You're *going*. Uncle Paul's going to take you. That's final."

So I went to the banquet with my uncle Paul and my cousin Bill. Bill was a great kid and we were born two days apart, so it was okay to go with them; but I felt terrible all day. And when the time came to leave, I still didn't want to go, so I left for the banquet with a bad attitude. The hole left by my father's death made itself crystal clear to me that night.

I looked around at the tables in the room—father-son, father-son, father-son. I didn't hear a word Bob Feller said that night. I watched the tables, observed the other kids, and thought, *I wonder if that man is his father.* I knew many of them and I knew that I was the one without a dad. I was the one with a father-sized hole.

I went home feeling crushed. That was the first time I *knew* I was different. I felt as though people looked at me and whispered to each other, "Hey, *there's* the boy without a father." Today I understand those conversations took place only in my imagination, but at the time they sure felt real.

That evening, I looked around at the family pictures in the

banquet room. I stared at the fragmented picture at my own table—and I saw a big hole where my father should have been.

I just had to fill that hole.

◼

I stayed home a lot the summer after Dad died. I didn't want to go out and I didn't want to do much of anything. My cousin Jim loved to fish. He was always getting a group together to try its luck at the dam. But I'd lost all interest in fishing. When Jim said, "C'mon, Gottfried, let's go fishing," I thought, *That's the last place I want to go.*

The truth was, I barely knew how to fish. When I'd gone with Dad, he baited my hooks, freed my line when it got hung up in the weeds, took the fish off the hook, and gutted and cleaned it. I hadn't learned much of anything about the whole process.

So I quit fishing. That summer I made a decision: "I'm never going fishing again." I still don't know how to fish; truthfully, I've hardly tried. I took my daughters once when they were younger, but it was a disaster. I didn't know what I was doing and the whole time I thought of Dad.

◼

My dad's death made we swear off fishing, but how do you swear off wearing ties? One day early the next year I had to put on a tie for some event at school.

"I don't know how to tie this tie," I told Mom as the father-shaped hole hit me once again. Dad had always tied the tie around his own neck first, then put it on mine.

"Go ask Joe," Mom suggested.

So I went to Joe and told him, "I don't know how to tie this tie."

"Give it to me," he said. He took it, tied it on himself just as Dad used to, took it off, then put the loop over my head and around my collar. As he tightened it up, he said, "Someday, when we have some time, I'll show you how to do this."

But he was always too busy, and then he went off to college. So he never did teach me. Really, I never *wanted* to learn. For me, it was a symbol. Every time I had to wear a tie, I thought about my dad not being there to teach me.

I still don't know how to tie a tie. My wife, Mickey, ties them for me.

After Dad died, I felt lost. I kept asking *Why?* and *Why now?* I couldn't concentrate on anything. Although everyone else in my family seemed to be doing okay, I lost my motivation, felt terrible, and continued to grapple with knowing that Dad wasn't coming home again.

I just didn't care about school. I became more introverted and kept pretty quiet. I'd lost the one person I could really talk to, the one person who would answer any question I had—and I was losing myself, too. The darkness that came slowly over me was getting more pervasive, and I couldn't find a way out of it.

But Sister Kathleen—my sixth-grade teacher at St. Joseph's—saw the darkness. The year after Dad died, she spent extra time with me. She helped me realize that life would go on. It wouldn't be the same and it would never be as good as it used to be, but it would get better.

She seemed to know what I was going through. Without her gift of time, I don't know if I'd have made it through that dark season. Sister Kathleen would sit with me, pray with me, and talk about the Bible. She taught me what it meant to have a relationship with Jesus Christ. One day she read a verse to me from Jeremiah:

"'I know the plans I have for you,' declares the LORD, 'plans to prosper you and not to harm you, plans to give you hope and a future.'" (Jeremiah 29:11)

Scripture has the power to change a person, and that verse stuck with me. It didn't take away the hurt and it didn't fill the hole, but it made sense to me and pointed the way out of the darkness. It brightened my situation.

Sister Kathleen also explained what it meant: "The Lord is looking out for you, Mike. "He's not going to let you go. He's got a future for you, a future of blessing. And you will see your dad again."

There I was, at the roundhouse of the tracks of my life, with countless directions facing me. Sister Kathleen had given me a choice. I could go on, living in bitterness and letting the loss of my father claim me or I could decide to trust God's plans for good in my life.

I made a decision that day. I was going to see my dad again

and I would make it through. Despite the pain, God had a plan.

■

While the gap in my heart brought pain, the search to fill it provided a perspective that God saw fit to nurture and use. Without the emptiness, I doubt I would have had the necessary perspective. And without that perspective, I don't think God could have used me in the ways he has.

Along the way on my search, different people began to stand in at the empty place of my life, and they showed that a little attention, affection, affirmation, authority, or acceptance can make a difference to a boy without a dad.

In Crestline, Hump Hagen was a fixture at the athletic fields. Hump (short for Humphrey) came to all the games he could, and retirement gave him a lot of extra time. He would sit behind home plate in an old, web-back lawn chair. He had earned the respect of the community, and I knew his reputation and had seen him at the games.

When I was twelve years old, I was the catcher for the baseball team. One night I caught a good game and we won. In those kinds of moments, I felt Dad's absence in a profound way. If he had lived, he would have congratulated me, told me I'd done a good job, and expressed his pride in me, the way every father should.

After the game that night, while all the other boys joined their dads, I was packing up to go home. Hump walked over to me and threw me a brand-new baseball. "Mike," he said, "I wanted to tell you, I really enjoyed watching you play out there tonight. You really hustled." And he gave me a pat on the back.

It was a little thing in the big picture, but it made a huge difference to one boy. Hump Hagen figured I could use some attention, some affirmation, some affection, and he gave it out. He saw a hole and he attempted to fill it.

That's why I try to look out for boys without dads. I get a lot of promotional giveaways in my work for ESPN and GMAC—such as balls and jerseys and lamps and T-shirts. Every time I'm with a boy, I give something away. And I put my arm around him and tell him he's doing a great job. I want to be like Hump Hagen, making a difference to one boy.

Even when I went off to college, people from Crestline saw the need and tried to help. A good man in town by the name of Herb Morton called my mom just before I finished college and asked, "Is Mike going to graduate with a suit?"

"No. He doesn't own a suit, and I can't afford one," she replied truthfully. "He's going to wear a white shirt and a clip-on tie."

"Mrs. Gottfried, I don't want Mike to graduate in a shirt and tie," declared Mr. Morton. "He needs a suit. Would it be all right if I helped him get a suit for graduation?"

Herb Morton sent me one hundred dollars to get a suit. "Someday," he said, "I want you to do the same for someone else."

I took him seriously. These days, I buy suits for boys who don't have one, so they can graduate with a suit. And I tell them that someday they need to do the same thing—buy a suit for a kid who can't afford one. I've bought *a lot* of suits. In fact, the local men's store in Mobile gives me a call when it has a sale, and I call one of the boys and have him meet me down there, and he walks out with a suit.

A Herb Morton suit.

◾

All through my high school and college years, things did get better. The loss I felt changed from something that could have devastated me to something that I always felt, but that had no power to harm me, unless I let it. I had chosen to believe God's promise.

When my dad died, the devil wanted to jump into the picture. He wanted to place influencers in my life—people and things that would take the place of my dad and turn me toward sin. He wanted me to head down ugly and worthless tracks. He wanted to catch me at the weak place, the hole my dad's death had left inside me. I was under attack, even though I didn't know it at the time.

But God was there, too. He wanted to fill that hole with good things and good people. He wanted to make sure that, despite the painful gap in my family picture, I could learn to trust him with my future. I could believe that he would help me find a way to fill the hole—not completely, but enough to make a difference.

That's why I tell boys, "It's always going to hurt. The hole in your heart will always be there. You'll always feel the loss of your dad. You're not going to get over it. But you're going to get better. It does get better."

And that's the truth.

FILL THE GAP

Psychologists say that at age four or five, children have a "bubble of emptiness." If they do not hear that they are loved—if they are not affirmed and the pattern continues—then they grow up with a hole. They feel empty and driven to fill the void with anything that offers the promise of validation: family or fear, grades or gangs, school or drugs.

God designed moms and dads to fill the void to the best of their ability, with God's help. But when one or both parents are missing, that bubble has a hard time getting filled.

Over the years, I have come to see that the most glaring vacuum in a fatherless boy's life takes the form of the five father-functions. At Team Focus we did not set out to aim precisely at these five elements of a father's influence, but whenever our attempts succeed, it's because we provide these five things that every boy craves from his dad.

Now I'd like to take a closer look at *affection*, the first of the father-functions. And I'd like to show you how a rich supply of it can make all the difference in the life of a fatherless boy.

One of the hardest things we do is to let go. That's true as a parent, and it's also true at Team Focus, especially at the end of a camp. We get attached to these guys and we know some of them don't go back to great situations. A lot of times the boys don't want to go home.

On the last night of a camp in Maryville, Tennessee, I was getting ready to speak at the awards banquet. Just before my talk, I got a call on my cell phone from Frank Modarelli, a worker in the camp.

"We've lost a boy," he admitted. "We can't find one of them."

"What?" I exclaimed. *Could I have heard him right?*

"We've lost him," Frank repeated. "It's Tim."

"How could you lose a boy?" I demanded. I had a hard time believing it.

"We'll find him, Coach, I'm sure we will," Frank reassured me, "but we wanted you to know we're one short right now."

I ended the call, then stood up to give my talk. Immediately after finishing, I called Frank back.

"Did you find Tim?"

"I found him, Coach," Frank replied. "He was hiding under the bed. He doesn't want to go home."

Later I found out the reason for Tim's odd behavior. He lived in a bad neighborhood with a family in a rough financial situation. We also discovered that Tim's brothers were beating him; the bruising and the pain had become daily. At camp he felt safe, was getting three meals a day, and received the loving care of godly men who showered him with hugs and encouragement.

Most of the boys in our program do not live in abusive situations like Tim. But boys without fathers have a huge disability stemming from an acute lack of fatherly affection. Moms can step up for some things a boy needs, but no one—not one other person on earth—can hug and kiss a boy like his father. And some of those fathers don't do it or aren't around to do it, or they hurt their sons instead of hugging them.

In our first or second year into this ministry, Mickey and I realized that a simple touch from a man frightened some of our boys. They'd grown up with abuse, so they would pull back from our team. That surprised us. We learned to approach the boys slowly and with discernment. But once the wall comes down, those same boys reveal an intense hunger for a man's affection.

I tell the boys in Team Focus all the time, "When I see you, I'm going to give you a hug." It's a matter of fair warning.

But often they look at me as if I have two heads. "Hey," they object, "that's a hugging thing. That's for sissies."

"Listen," I reply, "you're on a team. What do teams do? I'm going to tell you what they do. The Pittsburgh Steelers, they win the Super Bowl, the clock runs out to zero, and what do they do? They run to each other and they hug each other. At a baseball game—Atlanta Braves and the New York Yankees— in the seventh game of the World Series, John Smoltz strikes A-Rod out for the last out in the ninth inning, and Atlanta wins. What happens? They all run to the mound and they're all over each other, hugging each other. Why? Because they're a team.

"Those players bleed together and they laugh together. They've lived together and they'll die together. They sing together and they cry together. And when you get like that as a team, you *have* to show the affection. It's part of being in a family."

I do not warn the boys in vain about my hugging them! I'm always hugging these guys. Once they get used to me, they just come up to me with their arms out, ready for a big bear hug.

Usually, on the last night of camp, boys tell their stories. I start with mine. I talk about losing my dad and I tell them how I felt. I let them know how many nights I cried, and I tell them the truth about the place in their hearts where they'll always have a hole. I nearly always break up in front of them (at least a little) because the pain of losing your dad never goes away.

My tears invariably prompt other tears, and pretty soon guys are forming little groups—hug huddles. Men counselors get in the middle of it all, and it is good.

Really, really good.

Dear Team Focus,

I spoke to you when I called to sign Ben up for camp. Ben had just lost his dad and I was concerned about him not accepting it.

Ben hadn't seen his dad but twice in the last four-plus years. His dad has been in jail since he was two. What was so hard for Ben was that he was supposed to visit his dad the day he passed away, but he wasn't able to make it and was planning a visit for the day after. I think that's why it was hard for Ben to accept, because he felt guilty that if he had gone as planned, he would have gotten to see his dad for the last time.

Ben told me that at camp he broke down and

cried and told me everyone cried with him and that a lot of kids had lost their dads or were abused by their parents. When Ben came home from camp, he finally read the sympathy cards and I could tell he was on his way to healing.

Ben speaks about all of you with the highest regard. Again, thank you for making a difference in Ben's life and being the blessing Ben and I both needed.

Melissa Jackson

CHAPTER FOUR

LOOKING FOR
ROLE MODELS

I n my search to fill the father-shaped hole in my life, I began to closely observe men. Of course, some great women also influenced and taught me. But the shape of the hole left by my dad was unquestionably male, and that's what I needed to fill the gap.

Of the men who most influenced me and served as role models, the majority were coaches. For other boys, it may be teachers or pastors, relatives or neighbors. But for me, coaches filled the place my dad left. That makes sense, because he was a coach at heart; that's the way he parented. He saw his role as an encourager, a person to hold you accountable, teach you the right way, then cheer you on to do it. So I looked for other men who could do the same thing.

I made a point to study them. I would ask myself, "Do the players under him respond to his leadership? What makes this person good? What makes his life worthwhile? How does he help other people? What is it about him that makes people respect him?"

I noticed some people who couldn't get things done and who didn't have the respect of those who worked with them. I decided early on not to spend time analyzing why these men *didn't* succeed. Instead, I purposefully looked for men who pulled it off. I paid attention to *what made a difference.* I noticed that these people invariably offered something extra, something more. It might be a touch, a word, a smile—something that affirmed and challenged you, made you reach higher. It might be a hand on the backside, or just saying, "Good job." It might be a certain attitude, or a way of relating to others. I looked at what really worked to change other people. What would pep you up and give you what you needed to keep going, keep striving?

I did this because I believed God had plans for me, and those plans would place me at the right time and the right place with the right people. Each of these men made a dramatic difference in me, and they lifted me to the next level. Each of them, in distinctive and special ways, helped stand in for my father by supplying some of the five father-functions missing in my life.

God says, "I know the plans I have for you." And he means it! From my days growing up in Crestline and throughout my college years, he put me in direct contact with the right environments and individuals who would have a real impact on my life.

Coach Merle Hutson

Talk to just about anyone from Crestline, and it won't take long before one name gets mentioned as the local hero: Coach Merle Hutson. No one ever used his first name, and his last name was unnecessary. Everyone in town called him Coach. Crestline had many other coaches in the schools and in the kids' leagues, but only one person qualified to bear the single title.

Merle Hutson was Coach.

The football stadium at Hamilton Park now bears his name. Everyone who grew up in my hometown from the 1930s to the 1990s knew Coach, and most bear his stamp of character, encouragement, and excellence.

Coach Hutson and his wife, Peg, never had children, which probably motivated them to invest their lives in the children of our town. While the Hutsons did not leave a family legacy in the usual way, they left a dramatic legacy in the lives of uncounted Crestline families. And that legacy has traveled around the United States and the world.

Here is an amazing fact: Crestline, a small railroad town in north-central Ohio that in Coach's day had a population of around five thousand, has produced an estimated *one hundred* coaches, some of whom have coached major schools and teams. Sons, grandsons, and great-grandsons have continued the tradition. And there are plenty of women coaches, too. It's simply a social phenomenon.

When you ask townspeople, "What is it about Crestline that produces coaches?" you get a quick and consistent answer: "Coach Hutson." Ask the town's coaches the same question, and to a person you will get the same answer. Coach Hutson's legacy has permanently altered the destiny of both men and women in my hometown.

Both John and Joe DiPietro became coaches; John says it was because of Coach Hutson:

"I think I can say he's the model of what every coach should be. He was strong. He was fair. He was loving. He was tough when he had to be. Very caring. When I talk about him I get goose bumps—just talking about him. That's the truth. And I think he put a lot of us kids on the path to coaching."

My brother Joe has served as athletic director for the University of South Alabama for twenty-four years. "Every child in town wanted to be coached by Coach Hutson," he says. "I never got a chance to have him coach me directly, but he was a constant presence whenever kids were playing in town."

My nephew Mark, Joe's son, was born in Crestline. He's the head coach for the University of Alabama's Crimson Tide basketball program. Jack Harbaugh, my cousin who lived down the street, has enjoyed a long career as a coach. He was an assistant at Iowa, at Michigan, and at Stanford and served as head coach at both Western Michigan and at Western Kentucky. At the latter school his team took the 2002 NCAA Division I-AA national title.

Jim Harbaugh is Jack's son. You may remember him as a three-year starter at the University of Michigan under Bo Schembechler. He began his pro career with the Chicago Bears as a first-round draft pick in 1987 for Mike Ditka. After fifteen years in the NFL, Jim started coaching, first as quarterback coach for the Oakland Raiders, then as head football coach at the University of San Diego. Now he's starting his first year heading up the football program at Stanford. Jim's brother, John, has coached in the NFL for nine years as special-teams coordinator for the Philadelphia Eagles. John worked for me when I was at Pittsburgh in the eighties. Both John and Jim, as well as every other coach who has come out of Crestline, trace their coaching heritage to Coach Hutson.

Coach was a big man: six feet two inches tall, and around 210 pounds. He came to town in 1932 with a reputation for football, playing three years at Heidelberg College as an all-Ohio tackle. Rumor had it that he had played football for the Cleveland Rams. He worked for the public school, teaching and coaching, and eventually became a vice principal. He served in the U.S. army during World War II in North Africa and Europe. When he returned home, he resumed his coaching and teaching duties and became the school's first paid football coach. He retired in 1974.

Coach Hutson was neither soft nor weak. He could be tough when he needed to be, but he was the nicest man you'd ever want to meet.

High school athletes who played football for Coach remember the quarter he gave to every player who traveled to an away game. Today you probably couldn't do that, but in those days it was just his way of saying thank you. If you lost the game, you still got the quarter—but there was no laughing on the bus ride home. It wasn't allowed.

Coach Hutson not only helped with the boys in town, he also assisted the girls. He taught them swimming and helped coach their sports. Many boys and girls learned how to drive from Coach Hutson, who taught driver's ed courses. He made sure every girl had a date for the prom—he liked to play matchmaker. If a girl wanted to go to the prom but didn't have a date, he made sure someone would ask her out. Coach Hutson coached life, not just sports.

By the time I played school sports, Coach had officially retired from public school coaching. Still, he remained active. He coached the summer baseball leagues. He continued to teach driver's ed and taught swimming during the summer at the Kelly Park pool, where he ran a concession stand offering candy and pop and other goodies. He seemed to show up at any game being played anywhere in town. Coach would umpire, coach, and give a running commentary on the games behind the pitcher's mound. We all learned the fine points of sports from Coach.

To this day, whenever I play baseball with my family— sometimes in the family room of our home—I officiate, coach, and announce from behind the pitcher in the exact way as Coach Hutson. All who saw Coach do it have mimicked him in their own sandlot games. His example continues even today to influence people in this and so many other things.

Influence—that's what I learned most from Coach Hutson. The way he handled himself, the way he treated kids, the way he garnered respect from adults, all of these things modeled for me how to effectively influence the lives of those around you. I saw through Coach that a positive influence is a powerful thing.

In the summertime we'd all head out on our bikes or on foot to the park, about a mile away, for baseball. The Big South Side team would play first, and the Little South Side team (my team) would play after them. Coach hung around for every game. On really hot days we'd play three or four innings, and then he'd take us all over to the swimming pool for a refreshing dip. We'd be with Coach every day in the summertime.

Parents had complete confidence in his teaching their kids to swim, since he'd already taught most of *them* to swim. They'd sign up their kids in the spring and send them to the pool for lessons in the summer. He would give a lesson, then stand outside the pool or sit on a bench and watch his students in the water. He taught the whole town how to swim . . . except for me.

Mom would give me money for a lesson and a pop—five cents for the pop and ten cents for the lesson. But I'd use it just for pop. I didn't care about learning how to swim. So I'd get two extra pops (Royal Crown) and go sit on the bench and talk to Coach while he coached the other kids how to swim. I don't think he ever figured out that I wasn't taking swim lessons. Maybe he knew it, but if so, he didn't let on. I just loved being around him and would sit and talk to him for the longest time.

I never did learn how to swim. In fact, I never even got into the pool. I would just sit and talk, soaking up Coach's attention. Later on, when maybe I was finally ready for a lesson, everyone else had advanced so far in their swimming skills that I couldn't catch up.

I craved attention from a man, and especially a man like Coach, and I felt content simply to sit there. While the other kids soaked in the water, I soaked up the positive attention of Coach Hutson. My mom could say to me all day, "Hey, you're doing a good job," but I was searching for somebody else to say it—someone like my father.

Coach would put his hand on my shoulder and instantly I'd think, *Boy, I made it today! I got Coach Hutson to put his hand on me.* Just a smile, a nod, a word of encouragement from him, made all the difference. Sometimes people will tell you you're doing a great job or you're a great guy or you made a great play, but you can't necessarily believe it. You question the person's motives. But when someone like Coach Hutson complimented you, you could take it to the bank. He meant what he said and you could count on it. I think everybody hungered for him to say, "Hey, you're pretty good," or, "You did a good job." It meant so much, coming from a man like that.

One time I was pitching in a baseball game and Coach saw

something that seemed not quite right, so he came out to the mound.

"Something wrong, Mike?"

"No, sir, Coach."

"You're all right?"

"Yes, sir."

He must have seen me twitching or moving a certain way.

"You gotta go to the bathroom?"

"No, sir." But he knew otherwise.

I didn't want to come out of the game because I knew what would happen if I had to take time out to take care of business. *If I leave here right now,* I thought, *somebody else is going to replace me and I'm not getting back in here.*

So I stayed in the game . . . and promptly wet my pants. I threw some dirt on them to hide the truth, but Coach said, "I told you so."

"I'm just gonna keep going," I insisted.

"I know. You go ahead."

So I did. And it was all right.

Coach Hutson always made things all right. He had such a presence that when he walked with his wife down the town's streets, you always knew it was him, even if you couldn't see him clearly. Everyone would call out to him. "Hi, Coach!" "Nice evening, Coach." "What about that game, Coach?"

He encouraged everybody, not only with his words, but with his life and his actions. You never saw him say one thing and do another. He'd treat his wife with honor, open a car door for her, carry the bags for her. He would talk up to the girls, talk up to the boys. He never yelled and I never heard him curse in all my years. I never saw him smoke, never saw him drink, never saw him in a bar.

I always saw him doing things right.

He was everything you wanted to be yourself. People respected him, liked him, and wanted to emulate him. He was consistent in his words and in his life. He wasn't a certain way one day, and a different way the next. He was steady. Reliable. Faithful.

In all my years growing up in that small town—and remember, everybody knew pretty much all there was to know about everyone else—I never heard a bad word, an ugly rumor, anything at all negative about Coach.

Coach Hutson was my model for what I call positive coaching. He built boys up and never tore them down. If he saw a guy struggling, he'd help him, encourage him to get better, then teach him how to do it. "I'm going to be here after the practice," he'd say, "and I'll work with you."

And he did. If he said he'd be there, that's where he'd be. He'd stay with the boy, help him to hit the ball better, throw the ball better, or catch the ball better. He spent individual time with the kids, time he could have used doing something else.

As I studied this man, I saw something powerful that I could use: If you can stay positive, you can motivate. If you can motivate, you can improve. And if you can improve, you can win.

■

God put Coach in front of the whole town of Crestline and said, "This is what a man is supposed to look like. This is the way a man is supposed to treat people. This is a real man." Coach Hutson was God's lesson to us, lived out in flesh and blood within the hours of our days. And for many of us, the lesson took.

Coach was the first person in my life to help fill the father-gap. This happened naturally, since his life had been woven into the very fabric of our town. Coach was coach to all of us, and when my father-coach could no longer be with us, Coach Hutson was there. He wasn't Dad, but he helped to fill the hole. I didn't recognize it at the time, but Coach had great skill in all five father-functions—affection, attention, affirmation, authority, and acceptance—and he invested those elements into my adolescent life.

Coach and I kept in touch during my college years and after Mickey and I got married. When I started coaching high school, I'd come back and look Coach up and get his advice about coaching and about life. Here was a man I could trust, not only to point out stupid mistakes, but also to cheer me when I did well. Even when I became a college coach, I'd check in with him—and he'd already know what I was doing, how my team was playing, and how things were going. He'd know my wins and losses, and more important, he always seemed to know what I most needed.

The town of Crestline was his town—no, he *was* the town.

All of us who lived there benefited from his interaction with us. And the legacy continues today! Coach Hutson forever imprinted the town of Crestline with his own stellar character.

Some time ago the town organized a Coach Hutson Day. We all came back for it, coaches and ballplayers and former students from around the country, to honor the Coach. A couple of the guys and I started a scholarship fund in his name that continues to help kids pay for college.

Eventually he had to live in a rest home, and I'd go back to visit him—just sit and talk as we did in the old days. Since his passing, I drop by his grave sometimes to think, not because I believe he's there, but because it helps to talk things out as if he were. I'm not the only one; his grave gets lots of visits from the people he influenced over the decades.

This remarkable man coached a whole town and inspired thousands of people through his life and his words. Even when I moved away from Crestline and left Coach behind, his influence in my life lived on and drove me to find other men to help fill the gap.

College Coaches

I had one offer out of high school: a college football scholarship at Morehead State. Talk about the Lord putting me in the right place at the right time—that was it. Morehead was the right place for me to study and the right place for me to discover the men God would use in my life. I would never have guessed I would go to that college, but the Lord knew his plans.

How I ever got into that small Kentucky college, I'll never know. I didn't know anybody at Morehead and they didn't know me from Adam. It was a minor miracle that I got in there (if there are minor ones).

I was a good football player in high school. I played quarterback and we won again and again, but I had no idea if I was "good enough." Like a lot of kids, I didn't know what it took to get noticed, or how to get a scholarship, or whether I even qualified. Not one coach from Morehead ever came to see me play football—another part of the miracle. We did all our talking with the school and the athletic department through the mail. They sent me a letter in January of my senior year and I signed for the scholarship without ever visiting the school.

Joe had started at Kent State, but he came home after the first year, got married, and began attending nearby Ashland College. By living closer, he could lend a hand with Johnny and me and Mom.

In February of my senior year, Joe said to me, "We need to go down to Morehead and take a look at this place." So in March, Joe and I and my uncle Paul drove down there, got a hotel room, and Joe and Uncle Paul took me over to the college for a look. They didn't stay around, however; I was on my own.

I met with the admissions people. "What do you want to major in?" they asked. And I couldn't think of anything.

"Well, I want to be a coach," I said.

Armed with that information, they picked my major for

me: "Okay. History and PE," and that was that—I was a physical education and history major, same as most other athletes.

I walked around the campus, read some of the school's sports brochures, and saw the other football players. I learned who would play quarterback the next year—a senior named Paul West—and I watched for him. I learned he was a Big Man on Campus, team captain, dating the homecoming queen—a general Mr. Popularity. But I thought, *You know, I'm gonna be where he is. He doesn't know who I am, but I'm gonna have his job.* I wanted to become the quarterback of the team; that was my main goal. Nobody else needed to know it, but that's what I set out to do.

I also met with the coaches, all 150 pounds and six feet one inches of me—not what you'd call prime football material. After I left the meeting, the coaches probably looked at each other, shook their heads, and said, "*What* have we done?"

They told me I would have to run a fast mile, since no one could make the team without running a fast mile. So I returned home determined to train hard. I trained all through the spring and summer of that year. Joe would drop me off miles from home and say, "Okay, run back home." I trained the whole time with one thing in my mind: *I gotta be the quarterback.* I wanted Paul West's job and I worked hard to get it.

At practice that fall, from the first day we ran a mile, I beat everybody. From that time on, they had me spot other players who were having trouble making the mile.

Still, the coaches were not impressed. "Okay. He can run a

mile," they said. "But running a mile doesn't mean he can play football—and he can't play dead in a western movie!"

But I proved them wrong.

Despite my goal-setting bravado, the truth is, I was both green and nervous. My emotions swung back and forth between confidence and loneliness. I would practice and work hard and feel good about things, but at night, I'd start feeling lonely.

For the first time in my life, I was away from home, away from my family, away from the tight-knit community of the South Side of Crestline. I had moved just over the border in Kentucky, but I might as well have landed in Alaska. I was far away from where I belonged, I felt homesick, and I wanted to quit and head back to Crestline.

At the beginning of the season, they brought in a lot of numbers—that is, the recruiters filled up the rosters with plenty of players. The big numbers meant that not many guys were actually going to play; they would have to sit it out. Because of that, lots of guys quit and went home. They came to play, and if they weren't going to play, they weren't going to stay.

We started with seven or eight quarterbacks—and while none of the rest could throw, I could. As our practices got more intense, the others just couldn't get their passing games going. The coaches asked me to quarterback for the scout teams—the teams that scrimmaged against the first defensive team—so I got in some good practice every day.

I tried to make something happen for the scout team, get

something serious going. I played those practice games as if they were the real thing. You're really not supposed to do that, because the coaches want to build confidence in the first-team players. They want you to play to lose. But I thought, *Why should I do that? Why not win?*

So I practiced every day with Earl Bentley, the defensive coach, even though I was a quarterback. I thoroughly trained his defense. Every day, every week, I just kept making little goals: *If I can just make it through one week,* I thought. Then, when I'd made it one week, I'd set another goal: *If I can just make it through the first two weeks.* I kept setting goals like that, adding one little goal to another. Week after week went by, and I achieved goal after goal. I had made it a goal to make it onto the first travel squad, and I made it—yet another miracle.

But even as I achieved some success, I continued to struggle with the desire to go home. Kentucky might not be far away geographically, but it was a world away from Crestline.

On my first day at Morehead in 1962, I felt lost. I didn't know anybody. But soon I met a freshman football player, Reggie McGiniss, from Niles, Ohio. Reggie had played under Coach Tony Mason during his school's amazing forty-eight-game winning streak.

"Reggie," I said to him, "let's go downtown and have a Coke." Both of us had just arrived on campus and we didn't have practice until the next day.

"Yeah," he replied, "let's go."

As soon as we walked into a restaurant, a man ran up to me and said, "You can't come in here."

His words confused me, because the place was full of people.

"Are you open?" I asked.

"Yes," he said, "we're open, but not . . . look, you just can't come in."

Now I was really confused, so I asked, "Well, are you closed?"

"No, we're not closed, but you can't come in."

I just didn't get it. We wanted to come in and have a Coke, that was it. Finally, some guy saw our situation, must have guessed we were college students, and realized we were new to town. So he approached me, ignored Reggie, and asked me, "Are you a football player?"

"Yeah, I just got to town."

"You can't come in here with *him*," he replied, gesturing to Reggie.

"With who?"

"With *him*."

"Why is that?" I wanted to know. It still hadn't dawned on me that Reggie was black, I was white, and that the difference was a big problem for these people. "I don't understand this."

"Well, then," the guy sneered, "you just need to turn around and go back to where you came from."

"Okay," I said, and we headed back to campus. The incident stunned me—I had no idea such a thing could happen. I didn't know people could think and act like that.

I never gave that restaurant my business.

When our football team played in Tennessee, I remember members of the opposing team saying insulting, ugly things against the blacks on our squad. Even the fans shouted out mean things. It shocked me. "Can you *believe* this?" I'd say, looking around at my teammates. But everyone else seemed to understand.

In Crestline, I had never been exposed to the kind of racism that existed in the rest of the world. Some of my best friends growing up were black, and their race never made a bit of difference to me. So when I came face-to-face with bigotry, I wanted no part of it.

One of my best friends at Morehead was Howard Murphy, the first black football player at the school—and Morehead was the first nonblack midsouthern school to accept black students. In 1961, Howard Murphy earned all-conference recognition as a halfback. He was a good kid and a great friend and I spent a lot of time with him. In fact, at Morehead I spent most of my time with the black guys—I didn't know any different, and I didn't want to. Crestline had taught me to respect all people, and that conviction almost made me leave Morehead. But in the end, I stayed.

For the homecoming game my freshman year, Joe drove to Morehead to watch me play. He drove all night, about a five-hour drive—but not merely so he could watch me play.

Joe knew my struggle. I'd tell him, "Maybe I'll stay just

through the season," or, "Just let me finish up this year, then I'm coming home." I had determined I would not return to Morehead. I would stay for the football season—I didn't want to be a quitter—but I wouldn't be coming back the next year. I felt homesick for my mom and my town, and I felt better when I told myself that in just a few more months, I'd be home.

The same thing had happened to Joe, so he knew how I felt. But Joe was concerned for more than my homesickness. My brother had received a letter from my coach, a letter that he knew had the potential to speed my departure from college— something he wanted to keep from happening.

Joe was trying his best to be the father I needed. When he learned of my struggle, he wrote to the coach, trying to find out how I was doing. Before the homecoming game, Joe told me about his letter, then showed me the letter my coach had sent back.

"Mike's doing all right," the letter read. "He's a good player. We've decided we're going to redshirt him for the rest of this season." Redshirting is the practice of extending a player's scholarship for one year by not putting him in games his freshman year. Being redshirted is usually a good thing, because you get five years of scholarship to get your education and play your best ball. But it feels like a bad thing, because you know you won't be playing for a year. Instead, you'll just stay on the sidelines, sitting.

And now I was redshirted.

"Well, that's it," I told Joe. "I'm coming home."

"You come home, you'll have to get a job," he answered.

"I'm thinking about going back to Ohio to play. Somewhere close to home."

"You ain't quittin'! Never be a quitter," Joe said, using the very words my father had spoken to him on the last night of Dad's life.

That afternoon, I was on the sidelines with a pair of headphones on, keeping charts for the coaches. I knew I would not be playing for homecoming. By the fourth quarter, we had a solid win on our hands, up 24–0.

We were a good team on both defense and offense. We'd won some games, but our quarterbacks were weak at the passing game. They'd thrown only fourteen passes in the first four games of the season, an amazingly low amount. Our team could run the ball well, but we could not throw. And that made our stats look weak.

Through the phones I heard one of the assistant coaches, Roy Kidd, from up in the press box, talking to the head coach, Guy Penny, down on the field. They forgot I was also on the phones, and they began strategizing about how to play the end of the game.

"Guy," Kidd said, "we need to put Mike Gottfried in."

I perked up my ears and started thinking, *I just read Joe's letter, and I know I'm not supposed to be playing. I've been redshirted.*

"No, Roy," Coach Penny replied, "I want to redshirt him."

But Kidd insisted, "No, I think we need him. We're not throwing the ball very well and he's our best passer, even though he's fresh from high school. Let's put him in and throw the ball every play—get our passing stats up."

They still didn't know I'd heard the whole conversation on the headphones. I glanced over at the coach to see what would happen. He looked at me and shouted, "Gottfried! Get in there and start throwing!"

I could hardly believe it, but I got moving quick. "Okay, sir," I said.

Although the game was basically over already, new excitement filled the stadium; the crowd loves the drama of a passing game. I threw nine passes in a row and hit eight of them. We started on the 20-yard line and marched right down the field and scored a touchdown.

Let me tell you, I was happy! That was the greatest feeling, especially when I didn't expect even to get in the game.

My brother Joe saw the whole thing, and he knew I was going to be okay.

From that game on, the Morehead coaching staff revised their strategy and my red shirt came off. For the rest of that season, they started the first offensive series of each game with another quarterback, established a good running game, then brought me in for the second half to throw the ball.

That year we tied for the championship.

Yet with all the success of my freshman year, I still had no plans to return to Morehead the following year. I wanted to get into a school in Ohio.

When I went home for spring break, I told Mom what I

was thinking. She sounded a lot like Joe: "You've got to get a job, then."

That summer I returned to Crestline, got a job with the railroad, and made plans to give up my scholarship in Kentucky to attend a school closer to home. But by the end of the summer, I still didn't have a firm plan in place.

Coach Penny called and said, "Mike, you need to make a decision. You've got until tomorrow to come to school for practice—or your scholarship is gone." Even though I wasn't ready to make the decision, the next day I caught the train to Morehead and returned to Kentucky anyway.

I ended up staying the whole four years, playing football as the team's starting quarterback. And when I graduated, I knew I'd been with some of the best people I've ever met.

FILL THE GAP

If a boy is to grow up to be a real man, he needs the *attention* of a real man. And if a boy has no functioning father, he needs that attention from other men who will stand in for that missing father.

A couple of years ago I took Rueben along with me when I covered an LSU game with Auburn. I even got him into the LSU coaches' meeting. When Rueben sat down, I saw him get a confused look from Nick Saban, LSU's coach. *Who's the new guy?* Saban was clearly wondering. So I introduced Rueben to the coach and explained he was a Team Focus boy.

Rueben watched and listened intently the whole meeting. On the way out, he said, "Coach, I think Auburn's going to beat LSU."

"No, I don't think so, Rueben," I replied. I saw no way Auburn could win. The odds were against it and Saban seemed to have his team ready for a victory.

"No, LSU's going to lose," Rueben insisted. "Coach Saban is worried."

A little amused, I looked at Rueben and said, "Now, don't take all that energy in there for worry." Rueben had never been in a coaches' meeting and he obviously didn't know how it all worked. He was a rookie at this; I was the seasoned veteran. So I could tell him how it really was. "All of that energy is just what coaches do to get ready," I explained. "LSU's going to have a big win today."

That day Rueben got to work the field. He ran all over the place with our sideline guy, chasing down interviews and watching the on-field action.

Oh, by the way, LSU lost the game—but Rueben won. He got some real attention from a (humbled) father figure, something he really needed.

Every boy needs attention, including some who live near you. Fortunately, that attention can come in all sorts of ways.

When I'm covering a game for ESPN, I'll call the Team Focus boys who live in that city and get them together for lunch. I want to listen to them, talk with them, and get to know what's going on in their lives. I often arrange for them to visit the practices of football teams or to stand on the sidelines with me during a game.

The attention factor comes into play when I get to pull my contact strings and expose the boys to things they'd never have access to under normal situations. In that way, we can bring in some great men for the boys to meet at camps. A Camp Focus we held in San Diego is a good example.

Several prominent men popped in, unplanned, to say hello to the boys and give some encouragement. Steve Fisher, who coached the University of Michigan's Fab Five basketball team to victory, gave the boys a talk about diligence. Chuck Long, head coach at San Diego State (and formerly at Iowa), wandered in to say a few words, then stayed around to conduct mock interviews. Lynn "Red" Williams, a big guy who played for me at Kansas and went on to play for the Rams, the Raiders, and the Chargers, came by and impressed the guys with stories of being a gladiator on *American Gladiator's* and starring in *Mortal Kombat* movies.

God also works behind the scenes to provide serendipitous lessons for the boys. Once we took the boys to a Cleveland Cavaliers game and arranged to have them go courtside. We sat them all down on the game floor and I started to talk about their dreams, but it was hard to hear because someone on the other end of the court was dribbling.

I turned to one of my leaders and said, "Can you talk to him and see if he would stop shooting and dribbling the ball for a couple minutes so we can hear?" My leader complied, but he didn't walk to other end of the court to make a polite request; instead, he just shouted, "Hey! Stop dribbling that ball for a minute!"

The dribbler stopped bouncing the ball and immediately came striding over to us. I thought he was going to give us a rough time. He didn't.

"What's going on here?" asked Andre Miller, the best guard on that Cavaliers' team.

The leader who had shouted at him, now a little sheepish, explained who we were.

"So these are boys without dads?" Miller wondered.

"Yep," the leader answered.

"Let me talk to them." And then Andre told the boys his story, about growing up in Los Angeles with just his mom at home. *I* didn't put that moment together—God did. I guess God is concerned about showing boys attention, too.

In San Diego we took the boys to see the Padres play at

Petco Park. Jake Peavy, a pitcher from Mobile whom I've followed for years, arranged seats for us. He pitched for San Diego that night and the next morning showed up at camp to give out T-shirts and say a few words. He encouraged the boys to live out their dreams, and then he stayed around for lunch.

Can every dad provide something like this? Can every father figure? No, but that's not the issue. You can choose to show a fatherless boy that he's valuable and important by arranging for teachable moments. You may not be able to pull Jake Peavy into your house for a sandwich or arrange for your boys to meet a famous coach, but you definitely have ways at your disposal to show a young man how valuable he is to you.

One Sunday I had scheduled a restaurant meeting with two organizers of the GMAC Bowl. I took two of our boys to church first, Peyton and Jim, then brought them along to the restaurant. I sat them down at another table while I had my meeting.

"Okay," I told them, "you guys have been to camp. You know how to do this. You order on your own. Order whatever you want; you can take the leftovers home and share them." And then I left for my meeting at a nearby table.

Over an informal lunch I talked business with the bowl organizers, and as I was wrapping up the leftovers, the waiter brought over the tab. I picked it up and one of the men asked me, "How much is it?"

I looked at the total, a little perplexed, and reported, "Ninety-seven dollars."

"Ninety-seven dollars?" he repeated, a little shocked. "Give me that bill! It *can't* be ninety-seven dollars!"

He took the check and looked it over. "Here's the mistake. We've got the wrong bill. Whoever this bill belongs to, they ordered a lot more food than we did. And they had steaks!"

He called the waiter over and told him, "Sir, you gave us the wrong bill. This bill is too high. We didn't order steaks."

The waiter disagreed, "No, you have the right bill," then pointed to the table where my two boys sat. "Over there—*they* ordered the steaks."

Sure enough, Peyton and Jim had boxes and boxes of food packed up and ready to go. They had ordered enough for them, and then quite a bit extra to take home to their moms and brothers and sisters. They had taken my instructions seriously!

"Okay!" I said, laughing. "Looks like we have more work to do."

A father might teach his son all sorts of things, but it's far more than just knowing how much food to order, or how to politely tell someone to pipe down, or how to display some humility when you think you know what's what. Showing a boy some concentrated attention and teaching him important things (such as good manners) instills value in a boy and breeds confidence.

In part because of our efforts at Team Focus, we often see a radical change in confidence that comes to a fatherless boy. Self-confidence is hard to come by when your dad isn't there to give you a reason for it! But a faithful father-figure can choose to stand in the gap and make a real difference.

What would a dad do? That's the question I keep asking. A dad pays attention to his son. He knows what is going on in his boy's life and arranges to be there, to help. He makes special plans that tell his son that he matters, that he is valuable.

By giving a boy a little attention, *you* can help him know he has value.

Dear Team Focus,

Thank you, Mr. Rocky, Mr. Mike, and the rest of the staff members, for Team Focus. Thank you for taking your time to spend with me so that I could learn more about God and a new camp. I'm so glad that I was able to meet people beyond my wonders of meeting. This was the best camp I have ever been to in my life.

From: Eric

CHAPTER FIVE

MEN OF INFLUENCE

At Morehead I continued my search for men to fill the gap left by my father. By this time I was intentional about it—studying people, watching their behavior and their talk. Although I had plenty of subjects to study, four men most impressed me, each with his own personality and style. Those four men became stand-ins for my father, supplying the necessary ingredients to fill the father-void in my life.

Today, my life is what it is in great part because of these four men. They became my role models: Coach Guy Penny, Coach Earl Bentley, Dr. Adron Doran, and Dr. Jake Smith. These men shared several practical things in common, things I noticed right away:

1. I never heard them swear.

2. They always treated their wives with respect.

3. Each of them built up everyone around him instead of tearing people down.

4. God was important in each of their lives.

5. They didn't shy away from a touch.

While other men from my college days had a positive influence on me, these are the four who made the biggest effort and had the biggest impact. I studied them because they had "the right stuff" for coaching—even Dr. Doran and Dr. Smith, who weren't coaches by profession. I also studied these men because they provided things in my life that my father would have supplied had he been around. They filled the father space with good things.

Each of these men did their part, as if God had gifted them and put them in my path for just the right influence at just the right time. I could have gone either way in college; I could have followed the wrong people and gone the wrong direction in my eagerness to fill the gap. But in His grace, God provided four stand-ins who helped me through and encouraged me to head in a healthy direction. God placed me at Morehead under the shadow of these four men because it was part of His plan to give me a hope and a future.

Coach Earl Bentley: Affirmation and Affection

I found a man at Morehead who reminded me of Coach Hutson in Crestline. His style of coaching fit a different mold, but he was a positive guy whom everybody loved. Coach Bentley was always in church. He modeled what it means to be a Christian and a coach at the same time. He made a difference in my life by teaching me gentle affirmation.

Coach Bentley was an assistant at Morehead, specializing in defense. He also served as the track coach. At first, Coach Bentley called everyone by his last name—"Good morning, Mr. Gottfried," he'd say. It was his way of respecting us as men. But after a while, he gave me the nickname Fifteen, my number at Morehead. All through the years he's called me Fifteen. I'd call him up when I was coaching somewhere and he'd say, "Fifteen, how you doing?"

Coach Bentley employed some unique coaching methods. When I did a pretty good job of completing passes in our practice games, I ended up antagonizing the players on defense. Coach Bentley wanted me to get ready for what would come my way in real games, and he wanted to see if I could take the pressure of the quarterback position. So he told a big defensive lineman named Scott Davidson to hit me *hard*.

Now, in practice you're not supposed to hit the quarterback, but Davidson was just following orders. He hit me hard, just as the coach had asked him to, and he knocked me down. I got up, furious, and threw the football at Davidson as hard as I could, hitting him in the back of his head.

I did it before I thought about the consequences.

Davidson immediately came after me. Just before he let me have it, Coach Bentley stepped in between us. I thought I saw something in Coach Bentley's eye that communicated, "Hey, this guy's not taking anything off anybody."

That look explained everything. Coach Bentley wanted to see if I was tough enough. He wanted to know that I wouldn't take anything from anybody. Freshmen usually don't challenge the toughest guy on the team, especially by hitting him in the back of the head with the football. I think my teammates probably looked at me, too, and thought, *This guy's either nuts or he's got more than we've given him credit for.* Coach Bentley had made his point.

▪

Despite his unorthodox ways, Coach Bentley was a good coach and the players responded to him. He was funny and made everybody laugh. He cared about the players. But he also wanted to challenge a guy mentally to see what he'd do under pressure. Had he asked me to do anything, I'd have done it. And my teammates responded the same way.

One day during practice Coach Bentley said, "We're gonna practice tackling the telephone pole." I couldn't believe it. But they all got in line and he said, "I want you to put your shoulder into the pole and wrap up around that thing."

Jim Osborne was the first guy out. He ran as hard as he could and hit that telephone pole—and I tell you, his knees buckled and the pole shook. When he went down, I started laughing.

Coach Bentley just said, "Great job, that's a great job." Everybody else mumbled, "Oh, boy!" Osborne got up, staggered a little, and Coach put him back in line and said, "Oz, that was so good I want you to do it again." So Osborne ran up to the telephone pole—but just barely touched his head to it. Everyone broke out laughing.

"You sorry devil," Coach said—one of his favorite expressions—and he laughed along with us. "okay. I guess that's the end of tackling the telephone pole. The pole won't last." But Coach Bentley had accomplished his purpose. He saw that Jim Osborne, and all the rest of us, would do just about anything he asked us to do.

We enjoyed playing for Coach Bentley. He was fun. He had a way of doing things differently to make practice enjoyable. Beyond the fun of it all, however, was a man who cared deeply about his players.

In my senior year during a game with one of our big rivals, Western Kentucky, I had one of the worst performances of my college career. And Western Kentucky's players had told me it was coming.

As captain I led the pregame warm-ups and stood in the middle my circle of teammates. When our opponents came running by, one of them said to me, "You're gonna have a rough day." The comment was out of the ordinary, and I remember thinking, *Why would a guy say that?*

I soon found out why. By the middle of the game, they'd picked off *seven* of my passes. Every time they did so, one of them would come and stick it in my face: "I told you it was gonna be a long day for you, Gottfried."

Yet even though I'd gotten knocked around the field, we

were still in the game. Trailing 7–3, I walked off the field after the seventh interception, shuffled over to the sideline, and knelt down. I felt frustrated. Seven pass interceptions! That's almost a record, but one you don't want anyone to remember. I could not get anything going and I was down for the count.

The head coach, Guy Penny, stayed away from me. Everyone else kept his distance, too, figuring I just wanted to be alone—everyone except for Coach Bentley.

As I knelt there, I saw him come down the sidelines. He bent over and put his hand on my shoulder. I popped off my chin strap and took off my helmet and said, "Coach, maybe you ought"—it was hard to say it—"maybe you guys ought to try somebody else out there today." He knew how frustrated I felt, and I didn't know what to do except suggest a change of quarterbacks.

He put his hand on my back and said, "Mike, if we had anybody else, we'd do it. You'd be outta there. But we don't have anybody else and you gotta go back in." I looked up at him. He smiled and I smiled back. He pulled me up by my jersey.

So on the next series of downs, I went back in, hit a pass, and Tommy Gray did the rest. Touchdown! And we won the game.

Earl Bentley was not only my coach, he was also the professor for my kinesiology class, a course required for PE majors. One day I was only paying half attention when Coach Bentley announced to the class, "okay. For your final grade I'm gonna give you an activity. Your assignment is to do the activity, and then you have to write it out—write it up to explain what happened."

Coach then went around the room, handing out the assignments. "Alberts, here's what you're going to do: long drive on the golf course." Alberts wrote it down. "Baker, five low forward rolls." Baker recorded his task. "Gottfried, front flip off the diving board." And he went on to the next guy.

Now, Coach Bentley knew I couldn't swim. He knew I'd dodged swimming all through high school and college. But the assignment just passed over my head and I let it go. But finally it dawned on me: *front flip off the diving board!*

"Front flip off the diving board?" I said out loud. And then I did the dumbest thing ever—I raised my hand.

He saw my hand up and said, "Yes, Mr. Gottfried?"

"Coach, I can't swim! And you've got me doing a front flip off the diving board!"

He looked at me with a smile. "Nobody said you had to flip toward the water. Flip the other way if you'd prefer."

My face turned red. I went up to him after class to see if I could get him to change my assignment.

"You can do it, Fifteen," he said.

"I *can't* do it, Coach. I'll drown."

"You can do it. Just give it a try."

So I walked into the pool that day with the idea *I don't care if I drown or not. I'm gonna do this, because I don't want to let him down.* But the higher I climbed, the tighter my stomach got. I looked down, the ground and water fell away, and I just couldn't do it. I kept seeing myself in the water, sinking to the bottom like a rock.

I turned in a paper without doing the dive. "I wrote this up, Coach, but I couldn't do it," I admitted. I didn't want to let him down, but I just couldn't flip off that board.

And he let it go. He just smiled, put his hand on my shoulder, and said, "It's okay, Fifteen." Instantly I remembered my dad doing basically the same thing years before when I dropped a bunch of frogs.

Coach Bentley's smile communicated his affirmation, while his touch communicated his care. Through both he was able to reach into my life and fill some space in the father-void.

Coach Guy Penny: Authority

Guy Penny, the head football coach at Morehead, was the authority, the one in charge. He taught me what loving authority means.

Coach Penny was unlike other coaches I've known. He quietly studied both the sport and his team carefully and methodically. Yet no one doubted he was at the helm of the ship, the engineer of the train! He was a nice guy, kind to his players, encouraging, and everyone on the team knew he cared about them. But he was the one in charge—no questions. Someone had to be at the top of the chain of command, and he took his role seriously. Because of that, he inspired trust among his players and colleagues.

Guy Penny believed that the coach and the player ought to be separate. While Coach Bentley didn't mind having some fun with the guys, Coach Penny wanted you to learn respect for authority. He had no interest in being a pal to his players. He didn't try to act like us or try to come down to our level to get the best from us. He didn't have to do that. He knew that if he showed loving authority, we'd step up and give him our best. And he was right.

He intended to teach us that authority unleashes confidence. And more than the words he used, his methods demonstrated authority.

The last game of my freshman year, we were going up against Eastern Kentucky. On Monday before the game, Coach Penny watched as we stumbled through practice. It was not a pretty sight and we were not performing up to our abilities. After just a few minutes, Coach knew he had to do something. He called everyone over to him and said, "Okay, gentlemen. Go back to the locker room and get cleaned up. We're done for today."

We stood there in disbelief. What was he doing? He certainly had our attention.

"I'm serious," he said. "There is no sense in practicing if this is how you're going to do it. So no more today. We're done. We'll try again tomorrow."

We hit the locker room, but quietly. The next day we came out ready to practice and willing to work hard.

Coach Penny had a way about him, a confident authority, so that when he said something, you paid attention. You stepped up and came through.

His style of leadership meshed with our team. It gave us confidence that he was THE COACH. When you know you can trust your leader and the leader knows his role, it naturally instills confidence in you. Loving authority builds self-assurance—something I desperately needed when I first arrived at Morehead.

As I said earlier, those first weeks and months at college were tough. I got homesick, and although I worked my tail off at practice, I knew I wasn't going to play since I had learned of the coach's plan to redshirt me. I was ready to quit.

Coach Penny tried to encourage me in his own positive way. He "coached up"; he never put players down or berated them or belittled them. I knew I was safe around him. He pushed me to succeed and move ahead, to get better every practice and every game. He encouraged me.

Encouragement supplies the core foundation for courage. If we were to believe we could make it as a team—if we were going to exhibit the bravery needed to win—someone would have to establish a solid and trustworthy foundation. And that someone was Coach Penny.

It's the same way with God. He loves us and cares about us enough to be in charge, whether we like it or not. And if we learn to trust Him, His authority in our lives can give us great confidence.

This 1954 photo is Mike's family before his father's death.

Mike and Mickey's wedding day in 1967.

Mickey, Morey, Mike, and Mindy together as a family in 1987.

Mike as the 1988 Pitt coach.

Bill Walsh, coach of San Francisco 49ers.

Mike and Mickey with basketball great, "Dr. J."

Mike, Mickey, and Dallas coach Tom Landry.

Mike with baseball legend Joe DiMaggio in 1986.

Mike with Gates Brown (farthest left).

Steve Spurrier, Ken Stabler, Mike, and Danny Sheridan.

Mike and Steeler coach, Chuck Noll.

A 2003 photo of Mike and his brothers.

In 1998 with Chicago Bears coach Mike Ditka.

Mike and close friend, Pete Rose in 1986.

Mike, Marey, Don Shula, and Mindy in 1998.

2005 National Team Focus Camp

Dr. Adron Doran: Attention

I have never met a smarter person than the president of More-head College, Dr. Adron Doran. A strong man, he could speak with confidence; he knew how to stand in front of a group, command their attention, and explain complicated ideas. Dr. Doran often showed up to talk to the team. It was the first time I'd heard someone so articulate, so right to the point . . . so intelligent.

The last game of my freshman year we played our rival, Eastern Kentucky. We had to win that game to force a tie for the championship. Guy Penny told me, "Mike, I don't know if I'm gonna play you today, because this is a rival game." I wasn't in his plans; he and his coaches didn't want to take a chance on my inexperience.

Eastern quickly surged ahead 13–0. In the second quarter, the coach finally put me in. We had the ball on our own 20-yard line, and on the first play I dropped back to pass. An Eastern defenseman broke through the line and hit me so hard I fumbled the ball. As I looked up from the turf, I saw the ball bouncing toward the end zone, with two Eastern guys running after it. It was clear they would recover the fumble, score, and put us behind 20–0.

But when both of those Eastern players went for the ball, the ball scooted out, and one of our guys recovered it at about the 2-yard line. So I was saved! Kicker Mike Brown punted it downfield.

As I trotted over to the sideline, Coach Penny said, "You

need to settle down." I thought, *Settle down? I've only been in for just one play!*

When we got the ball back, Coach let me back in the game. I threw a pass to Howard Murphy, who ran for a touchdown. After we kicked the extra point, we were down 13–7.

Our defense was playing well and stopped Eastern after just a few downs. Then we got the ball back on a punt. On the first play from scrimmage, I passed to Jack Smith, who scored a touchdown. With the extra point we were now ahead 14–13, and the future suddenly looked much brighter.

And that was it for me; I never got back in the game. I went in for three or four plays, and I was done. The season was over.

We ended up winning, 20–13.

■

The next semester the school hosted orientation and I attended the convocation, where Dr. Doran presented an address. I was starting my sophomore year and already we were into heavy practice.

As I sat there, listening to one of the smartest guys I had ever heard, I noticed him talking about determination. Sometimes, he said, when you think you're down and out and things look as if they're going against you, you need turnaround determination to keep pushing ahead.

In the middle of his speech, my ears perked up. He was talking about *football*—and more specifically, about the last football game of my freshman year, the game against Eastern

Kentucky. He told the story of my fumble and the four plays I quarterbacked. He said I had changed the game and turned a loss into a victory. He told the students and faculty that they needed to follow that example whenever they got behind in life.

I enjoyed being mentioned, of course, but I noticed something else about that speech. *This person,* I thought, *this very* smart *person, knows my name!* Dr. Doran knew my name and he knew me, even though he was the esteemed president of the college and I was a wet-behind-the-ears underclassman. It made a huge impression on me.

Dr. Doran taught me the value of attention. Every person needs it and every boy craves it, especially from his father— and more especially if his father is gone.

So I studied him. I got to know Dr. Doran and his wife, Mignon, who paid attention to students just as her husband did. Eventually I started to feel confident sitting down to talk to him. I'd see him around campus and he'd have a conversation with me; he always seemed to know what was going on with my life. I developed a great relationship with both him and his wife.

It means something special when a person like that—whom you know to be better than you, stronger than you, smarter than you—actually knows your name. And he knows about you enough to talk with you, encourage you, push you higher. He pays attention to you.

That's what a father does. He's smarter, stronger, bigger, better. He towers beyond you in wisdom and stature. But he knows your name—he gave it to you! And he knows who you are and what's going on. He cares enough to talk to you about it, ask about it. He takes the time to know you through and through. He pays attention.

God works the same way. He knows your name, too, and He knows all about you. Best of all, He cares.

Dr. Jake Smith: Acceptance

Dr. Smith was a dentist in Morehead, Kentucky. He loved sports and was a great supporter of all athletics at the college. He lived close to the school and took a special interest in me.

Early in my first year, he met me after a game and invited me and another player to his house for Sunday dinner. We accepted his invitation and got to know his kids and his wife. Before long, I started visiting the Smiths' house just to hang around them. They felt like family to me.

Dr. Jake took me in—adopted me, in a way. He invited me along on family outings. I became one of the Smiths. I had close to an open invitation to show up at his house for a meal or a snack. Sometimes he would call the dorm and leave a message for me that he was coming over to take me to get a sandwich. I don't know why, but he treated me like a son.

Dr. Smith showed his hospitality and his welcoming spirit in spontaneous ways. He brought sweet memories of my dad back to me, because he'd show up outside my dorm, honk his horn, and say, "Hey, Mike! Mike Gottfried! I'm heading to Cincinnati to the racetrack. You wanna go?" Or he'd show up unexpectedly with tickets to a ball game and take me and several of my friends with him. He was just like Dad—he always had room for one more, and he always had room for me.

As I look back, I've wondered whether Coach Penny or Coach Bentley or even Dr. Doran didn't approach Dr. Smith and say, "Hey, you need to keep an eye on this fellow. Help him out. Make him feel at home here. We want to keep him around." While that may have happened, his interest in me wasn't just a "job" to him or a task he took on as a school booster. Neither did his friendship and generosity end after I left Morehead.

After I began my professional career and started coaching around the country, he'd come to my games, even traveling to Southern California when I coached against USC (and beat them!).

Dr. Smith accepted me. He made me feel welcome and wanted. He helped me know that someone wanted me around and cared enough to invite me in. I was a part of his family.

That's what a dad provides for his children: a place to belong. Family means being accepted and loved. You have an open invitation to the table. You belong to someone.

Once again, it's the same thing with God. When we know Him, He accepts us and brings us into His family, where we can know we belong.

■

One of the hardest things I ever had to do as a coach was suspend a player or throw him off the team. When you do that, you have to admit you failed. You didn't reach him. You couldn't pull him up. I hated kicking guys off the team and I never wanted to do it. But I knew that if a guy was about to ruin the whole team—bring them all down along with him—he had to be separated out, for his own good as well as for the team.

I watched my mentors do this, and I wanted to handle it in the same careful way they had. This is when "coaching up" is the hardest thing to pull off, but it's also the best way to handle such situations.

At Murray State I had to throw a guy off the team. A guard named Reggie Pope wasn't cutting it academically, and all the help we gave him had little effect. I sat down with him one day and said, "Reggie, this is going to be tougher for me than for you, but I'm throwing you off the team and off scholarship." I felt awful, but I tried to do it in a way that would help him in the end.

Reggie responded well. He got his act together and kept working hard. Eventually he rejoined the team and got back on scholarship. In fact, he became captain of the team in his senior year, when we won a championship. Today he works in a prison, dealing with inmates. We've stayed in touch, and when I talk to him today, he credits his success to the time at Murray State when I got tough on him. He thanks me for showing the courage to make the tough call and says it made all the difference in his life. If I hadn't taken a stand, he says, he wouldn't have made it.

All four men who most influenced me in college were touchers. They'd touch you on the shoulders. They'd grab you by the arm. They'd hold you. They had a masculine way of hugging, a hold with a hard squeeze and a grunt, so that you had no doubt you'd been held on to. It could even hurt when Earl Bentley did it. Still, you didn't want to say, "Ouch!" Out of respect, you didn't want to respond like that—but his hugs felt good despite their intensity.

The lessons I learned from these four men followed me into my coaching career. I don't know how many times I'd do something just as Coach Penny or Dr. Doran had done it. Or I'd find myself treating someone in the way Earl Bentley or Dr. Smith always did. Over and over, in various situations, I'd apply a lesson from one of these remarkable men.

Remember how I threw seven interceptions in one game? That took place in 1965. Almost a quarter of a century later, in 1989, I was coaching at the University of Pittsburgh. In a nationally televised game against West Virginia, we were down 38–10, and we felt the pressure. Late in the third quarter, things weren't looking good. West Virginia had picked off our quarterback, Alex Van Pelt, five times.

In my headset, I heard my offensive coordinator, Paul Hackett, say, "Do you want to take Van Pelt out? Because we can't win this game." He wanted to save him for another day.

"No," I said. "Let me talk to him. Then we'll see about pulling him out."

Alex came from West Virginia and was playing his first college game in his home state. He felt nervous, miserable, and his team was getting pummeled by twenty-eight points.

"You wanted to see me, Coach?" Alex asked.

"Yeah, Alex," I replied, putting my arm around his shoulder. "Let me tell you something. One time, I threw seven interceptions in a game."

He looked at me with wide eyes—my admission clearly stunned him. He couldn't believe it, and he didn't know what I was getting to.

"You know what that has to do with you?" I asked.

"No, Coach."

"Alex, I'm hoping you break my record!" Then I looked him in the eye and declared, "I'm not taking you out." I smiled at him, gave him a pat on the rear, and told him to go back into the game.

He started laughing and walked away. And then he got hot. On the last play of the game, we came back to tie it, 38–38.

I didn't tell Alex that story just to get him going, although I hoped it would. I told him the story so that he could relax and not feel so frustrated and be so hard on himself. I wanted him to get over the hump.

If you've been paying attention, you know that I didn't come up with that idea all by myself! Some great people had mentored me and showed me how to coach with affection, affirmation, attention, authority, and acceptance.

And you know what? It works!

As a boy I wanted to be like my father, and after his death, Coach Hutson became a role model for me. As I studied Guy Penny and Earl Bentley, I knew I wanted to coach. All four men were coaches, and I wanted to become a coach, just like them. This is what I wanted to do. This was my dream.

Dr. Doran and Dr. Smith added their own unique influences. These men made me believe I could do it. I knew I could pursue my dreams. *I'm going to be all right coaching,* I thought, *because I've had these good guys in front of me.*

These men sewed hope into me. God placed them into my life so that they could take some positive thread, provided by God, and weave that thread carefully into the fabric of my life. When I look back, I see clearly the thread of hope that each one sewed in. They made it possible for me to be strong, to handle the hurt, to face off with difficult choices and decisions, to endure some hardships, and still come out all right.

Coaching was my dream. But it was hope, sewn into the fabric of my soul, that allowed the dream to take shape. These four men helped make the difference for me. They made sure I stuck it out through all four years of college. They filled an empty place in my life, the place of my dad.

And that's why, when I graduated from college and began a career as a coach, I took these four men along with me.

FILL THE GAP

A dad affirms his son, letting his boy know he is valuable and that he is here on this planet for a reason. When a boy has no father, his need for affirmation doesn't simply go away. A godly man has to step in from somewhere to provide it—and when he does so, it can make all the difference.

I know this, because a lack of affirmation has the opposite effect.

In grade school I thought I was the fastest guy on my baseball team. In one game I hit a ground ball to shortstop and tried to run it out, but I got thrown out. As I trotted back to the dugout, the coach said, "Gottfried, you're running like you have a piano on your back." Before that moment, I considered myself fast; maybe I was wrong. But after that comment, I was never fast again. Because my coach labeled me slow, I thought I was the slowest guy on the team.

Words either bless or bleed. What you say to someone can stick with that person for years as either a wound or an encouragement. A coach or a teacher, a pastor or a parent, has tremendous power in the words he uses. Coach Les Steckel, president of the Fellowship of Christian Athletes and author of the book *One Yard Short*, told me about an experience he had in college.

"I remember a coach at Kansas," he said. "I was running sprints one day and he was watching me. He said, 'Steckel, if you were in a race with a pregnant lady, you'd end up third.'

And I've never forgotten that." Les said the coach's unkind comment stuck with him all his life. He wore the label *slow* from that time on.

Boys need to be affirmed in both word and in deed. They need to hear with their ears and know in their heads that they have what it takes, that they have something to offer, that they can achieve what they set their minds to do. A significant person in their life needs to provide all of that—most appropriately, their dad, but in his absence, a mature male role model.

Affirmation gives hope if it comes from the mouth of someone who has authority and who knows you intimately. If it comes from a person with authority, then you know you can trust the information. If it comes from someone who knows you through and through, then you know you can have confidence. Affirmation gives hope, something every boy needs.

At Team Focus we believe in affirmation. We are constantly telling the boys they are good, they are handsome, they are special. We go out of our way to commend a boy when he does a good job. We talk the boys up to each other in public, making a big deal out of their accomplishments and successes. In each monthly newsletter we tell encouraging stories about what Team Focus guys all over the country are doing *right*.

Boys without dads are missing the key ingredient of positive affirmation from a father. Dads have real power in affirmation because they have both authority and familiarity. Without that person, a boy longs to hear that he has done something well; he wants to know that he has something of value to offer. So we're constantly throwing around compliments. We attempt to create as many moments of positive affirmation as we can, in ways that will count for a long time.

Last summer I saw the smallest kid in camp playing basketball. He was just a little guy, about nine years old. He was dodging through and around all the other kids and straining to get the ball high enough to reach the basket. On the same team was the heaviest boy in any camp we've had. Both of these guys were giving it their all, doing their best, and working it out. In the midst of all the dribbling and shooting, shouting and tussling, these two boys received words of encouragement and positive coaching from our counselors. When the game ended, each of these two boys, hot and sweating, came off the court with their arms around each other in congratulations.

That's why we call it *Team* Focus.

We also have the boys speak in front of each other. Public speaking is a big fear for everyone, but especially for many of these boys who've never been affirmed by a dad. Some boys have a really tough time with this. We ask them to first introduce themselves and then tell us what they're going to be someday. We want to know their dreams.

The boys come up individually and give their names and describe their futures. One counselor sits in the auditorium and gives a thumbs-up or a thumbs-down, depending on whether the boy speaks out with confidence or mumbles quietly. If a boy can't be heard, we have him try again. And when he nails it—speaks in a loud voice with his head held up confidently—everyone cheers and claps. Counselors on the wings of the platform give high fives and hugs to the speakers on their way back to their seats. We confirm the dreams of the boys, sealing their aspirations with affirmations. We let them speak out their God-given dreams, because there is power in proclaiming the desires of your heart—and affirmation seals hope deep inside.

The hope that affirmation provides comes not only through words, but through actions. At Team Focus we attempt to back up our words with activities.

We like holding our camps at colleges because this gives our boys hope that one day each of them can attend a college himself. The college setting helps to set a boy's aspirations high, and being on campus, staying in the dorms, and eating at the cafeteria gives the guys a feel for what it's like. I tell the boys, "Look. Someone has told you or might tell you that you can't make it here, that you don't belong here. But I'm going to tell you, you *can* do it. You can do this."

Holding camps at hotels affirms the boys in other ways. Some of these kids have never been on a vacation and have never stepped foot inside a hotel. We once held a minicamp at a hotel in Ohio. One boy came to see me the second day and said, "Mike, I never knew what a hotel was. This is the first time I ever been in one."

We also affirm our young men by bringing in speakers

who will challenge and stretch them, speakers nationally recognized in their fields. Just being exposed to greatness can instill the value of achievement and effort in a boy. It might be a senator or a pastor, an athlete or an actor, a teacher, doctor, businessman—we have great people who come to share their stories. Someone who tells the truth about his life and lets you in on the secrets of his success, and who honestly describes his own struggles as a boy, can give a young man hope. He can go back home, even to a bad situation, and still carry hope with him.

At a Washington, D.C., camp, we arranged for the Secret Service to take the boys on a private tour of the agency's training camp. Normally the Secret Service does not give civilians tours of its facilities; it's just not open to the public. But God blessed, and they opened the camp to us. The boys thought it was great, and so did the Secret Service agents. They loved our boys.

They showed them all sorts of things. We went out to the training track where they teach agents how to drive the getaway car for the president. They let our guys take turns riding in a car while they backed up going 50 mph, doing "J" turns, weaving in and out of obstacles. You just can't buy that kind of experience—and none of us will ever forget those memories.

We decided afterward that we should invite some law enforcement officers to help at all of our camps. Some of these boys know law enforcement personnel only from the times they see someone hauled away in handcuffs, whether from the neighborhood or from their front porch. For some of our boys, the ones hauled away have been their dads. So it's good for the boys to see a policeman as a real person, a real man who can laugh, smile, and care about them.

We think the most affirming thing we can do for the boys is to introduce them to the love of God found in the person of Jesus Christ. That's why there is no more important time of day at a Team Focus camp than when the boys open up a Bible or sing a song or pray. We know that God is the primary source of love and that only in Christ will any boy be able to realize his ultimate destiny.

We offer no apologies for making Jesus Christ, the Bible, and faith in God the most important things we talk about. If we are concerned about the life of a boy who doesn't have a functioning father, then we feel compelled to show that boy the love of Christ. In our attempts to affirm a young man, to speak into his life and give him hope, we must tell him about God and explain the grace of Jesus.

We want the boys in our program to know that the Bible has every answer for every situation they will encounter. And we want them to know they have a Father in heaven who knows their name, understands their thoughts, bottles their tears, and loves them unconditionally.

On a typical camp day, the boys spend a half an hour every morning with a pastor—often Pastor Rey Dempsey, who has a heart for these young men. Rey teaches the Bible and the boys are assigned verses of Scripture to memorize each day. Throughout the camp we invite pastors to speak, many of whom have lost their own dad. Every evening ends with a time of worship and meetings in small groups where boys can open up and talk about spiritual things.

We figure that if showing affirmation sometimes means introducing the boys to famous, influential people, then how much more important to introduce them to the God of all the universe and His Son, Jesus?

In these ways, we try to sew hope into the lives of boys who don't have dads. In the few days they are with us, we want to affirm them enough so that hope becomes a part of them, stitched into their character and into their hearts. We know their hope will be tested and that rough circumstances will strain the fabric of their lives—but if we've done our work well, just maybe they won't come apart at the seams when bad things happen. That's the power of God-given hope.

Dear Team Focus friends,

I wanted to thank you so much for everything you all have done for Jim. Of course I love him and think he is special, but it warms my heart to know that you do, too. I sort of think of you as extended family because I know if something ever happened to me, you would be there for him. One can never have too many role models, and the mentoring that you provide just goes beyond words.

On Jim's return from the national camp he said, "When I leave Camp Focus, I feel spiritually super-charged." You are truly God's servants. Thank you and God bless you for the work you do.

Sincerely yours,
Victoria

CHAPTER SIX

TRYING MY
COACHING WINGS

'll never forget it. In fact, I remember it as if it happened yesterday. As we drove out of town on our wedding day, heading for our honeymoon, Mickey sat right beside me. I looked at her and thought, *How am I going to take care of her? What have I done? I can't take care of myself, so how am I going to take care of her?*

She's taken care of me ever since.

I wasn't ready to be a husband. I wasn't ready to be a father. And if my dad had been around, I think some of that would have turned out differently.

■

When Mickey and I got married, I owned three shirts, two pairs of pants, and a bunch of socks. Before the wedding, Mickey would try to guess which of the shirts I would be wearing when I came home from college to see her. What she ever saw in me, I'll never know.

Mickey and I first got interested in each other when she was a junior in high school in Crestline and I was a junior in college. We had known each other a little, about as much as people do who grow up together in a small town. Early in the summer between my junior and senior years at college, I saw her walking in downtown Crestline, and I determined to give her a call and ask her out.

On our first date, I invited Mickey to watch me play in a league softball game. Afterward we went out for a milk shake. How boring that "date" must have been for her! And how egotistical to think that watching *me* play ball might be something attractive and fun to do! It's a miracle that she agreed to go out with me. But it's an even bigger miracle that her parents let her go.

On a normal day, Mickey's parents would never have let her date a boy so much older. So when I first asked Mickey out, her parents called around town. It didn't take long to talk to the people who could give you the straight scoop; that's how small Crestline is. I must have had a good enough reputation, because they let her go out with me. Either that, or they talked to the right people.

Mickey was pretty, she loved sports, and she planned to go to college as a gymnast. She was easy to talk to and she enjoyed life. Once I got to know her, I knew that we could make a good team—and I suspected she would like being the wife of a coach.

■

Mickey and I dated in the summer when I came home to work on the trains. It was almost a given that I'd work on the trains. It was only too easy to find a job with Pennsylvania Railroad.

"Okay," Mom had said, "you've got to work at the railroad. Your father's friends and relatives who work there have called out ahead, and the guy is going to hire you for a summer job."

So I went out to the yard and met with the boss, who had been primed. All the pressure made it almost impossible for him not to hire me, and he seemed none too thrilled about it. He wasn't from Crestline and he didn't know me at all.

"You're going to be a brakeman," he announced.

I thought I would be a fireman; that's what everybody told me I would be. But I agreed to the new plan.

"You start tomorrow," he said. "Be here at nine." So that night I went home and told my mom, "I got the job. I start tomorrow. I'm going to be a brakeman."

Now it was Mom's turn to be not so thrilled.

"Oh, no, you're not going to be a brakeman!" she said. "Brakemen are always off the train." She knew brakemen had one of the most dangerous jobs on the railroad. "You'll get hit by a train, or something bad will happen to you. I'm going to call Bill Harbaugh." She didn't want to lose anyone else in the family, and she didn't want any more accidents. So she called Bill Harbaugh, who worked on the train, as well as another friend, and both went out to see the guy who'd hired me.

The next day I was a fireman.

For three summers I worked on the railroad. Every year I looked forward to coming home after school. It was a good kind of break.

Mickey lived on Pierce Street, across from a church and right next to the tracks. So when I was working on the trains, I'd have the engineer blow the horn when we passed her house. Sometimes she'd be out there, waving at me.

I learned how to "mark off," which meant not showing up to work and not having to go on a run. I didn't want to spend time away on the train when I could be with Mickey, so I'd call and say, "Hey, mark me off; I'm going on a date." I got marked off a few times (probably a few too many). Mickey says I could have worked real hard and earned a lot of money. But I traded some of that money for time with Mickey. I did what I needed to do to see my girl, the one I wanted to marry.

■

During my senior year I tried to see Mickey on the weekends whenever possible. I'd have to hitchhike home, but it was worth it. During the week I'd call her whenever I had the cash. I learned how to afford it.

My scholarship provided me free meal tickets for the school cafeteria. Meals were normally about two dollars, so I would sell my meal ticket outside the cafeteria—kind of scalp it—for one dollar. Then I'd go through the line with the people who bought it and pick up the food they pointed out to me. Then I handed them the tray of food, they'd sit down, and I'd beat it. I'd take their buck and get two slices of pizza and a pop for thirty five cents. Then I'd call Mickey at a pay phone with the remaining sixty five cents, which bought me three minutes to talk.

Soon I discovered a pay phone a couple blocks from campus that didn't work as it should; most of the time it gave back my sixty five cents. So I would call Mickey, and when the time ran out, I'd hang up the phone, and if it was my lucky day, coins would clink down into the coin return and I'd call her right back. Only I knew where that phone was, and I kept its location a secret. I didn't want someone to come along and fix the thing.

Just as Mickey got ready to go off to college, I proposed to her. She accepted and we set a date to get married in one year. But the timing was far from perfect! While I was ready to graduate from college, get married, and start a career and a family, Mickey was just getting ready to begin her own college education at Ohio State.

But Mickey understood my passion for coaching. She could see it and visualize us as a team. Crestline, with its emphasis on sports and teamwork, had prepared both of us for our dreams.

After graduating from Morehead, I got a job as a coach at Roseville High School in Roseville, Ohio. It wasn't my only option.

I had a contract to play for the Richmond Rebels in Virginia, part of the World Football League. I got all the way to the airport for the flight to Richmond, but I missed the plane. I'm glad I did.

I was also offered a high school coaching job at New Albany in Ohio. I seriously pursued it until they told me, "We're going undefeated whether you coach or the janitor coaches."

I was also ready to go to Central Catholic in Toledo as an assistant. It was a good program, but when the head-coaching job opened up at Roseville, I took it. I talked to a lot of people and many former coaches, and they all said, "Hey, if you can be the head coach, even if it's a bad program, you should take it. You can try out all your ideas—see if they work. You won't have to follow someone else's agenda." At Roseville I taught physical education and coached the football team, which wasn't very good. We won just one game that season and tied another.

As I look back on it, I think I could have used a year or two under someone else to learn more about how things really work. But I don't regret taking the job at Roseville. After all, it was close to Mickey at Ohio State.

■

Mickey and I were married the summer following her first year at Ohio State. She earned straight A's all through college, but because of my coaching and frequent moving around, it would be fifteen years and five schools before she would graduate.

After a year in Roseville, I took a job in Norwalk, Ohio. I wanted to get closer to home, and since Norwalk was about forty-five minutes from Crestline, I took the job coaching the

Flyers football team at St. Paul's Catholic School. It was another strong direction pushed by the Lord.

Mickey and I were a team from the very start. Since St. Paul's was a parochial school, and since it was located in a small town, and since Mickey had some experience with teaching and in those days you didn't have to be certified to teach, she got a job at St. Paul's, too, teaching physical education. We taught and coached at Norwalk for four years. Mickey and I were part of just a few lay teachers at the school; most of the teachers were nuns.

At St. Paul's, people knew and cared about football and we had great support for the program. I had a good staff, we were always ranked high, and we won a state championship. It became everything you'd want in a program, and we really enjoyed our time there.

We lived in a little trailer park. Since we weren't a whole lot older than our students, it was easy for us to get close to them. We always seemed to have a bunch of kids hanging out in the trailer.

We also had a little toy terrier named Max. The kids would call and say, "Hey, is Max home?" Mickey would look around and not find him.

"No, he's not here."

"That's because he's down here, at the town square. We're going to bring him home." That dog kept crawling under the fence to get out. But even if he did, so what? In that kind of town, you didn't worry much about it. Someone would always care enough to round him up and bring him home.

During our time in Norwalk, we reached one of the biggest milestones of our marriage: Mickey gave birth to our first child, Mindy. All the girls at school loved having a baby around. We did, too.

One day the nuns walked into my room at the high school and said, "You have to go over to the elementary school and teach first-grade gym." That's something I'd never done, and since Mickey already worked there, she offered her assistance.

"I've done this before," she said to me. "Do you want some help?"

"No," I answered, "I'm just going run a relay." I figured relays were always easy.

"They can't do it," she declared. "They're just first-graders. You'll have to teach them how."

I didn't believe her. Didn't *all* kids know how to run relays? So I had all the first-graders line up neatly, ready to start the relay. Mickey came over to watch the fun. "You all understand how to run this relay?" I asked, and they all nodded their heads. I had gone over the whole thing about ten times, showing them where and how to run. I figured they were all ready, so I blew the whistle.

And every kid in the gym ran in a different direction. I had a lot of work to do!

One day an administrator entered my room and announced, "The head nun is here from the diocese, and they need to check your lesson plans."

"Lesson plans?" I asked. I didn't use lesson plans; I just taught the kids on the fly. So later I went to Mickey and said, "I need your lesson plans."

"What will you give me for them?" she asked.

"I'll do anything you want me to do, just give me your lesson plans."

"You can't have my lesson plans. Just tell them that you teach by the seat of your pants." I begged her for those lessons plans, but she wouldn't budge. Finally, I promised to do chores for two weeks in trade. She gave me the plans.

And the head nun? She never showed up. I never had to use a lesson plan.

But I still had to do the chores.

■

As the high school's head football coach, it dawned on me one day that I had to win the rivalry game. Rivalries mean you're either going to keep your job or you're going to lose it. My friend at ESPN Lee Corso describes a rivalry game as a JS game—it's a "job saver."

One summer at Norwalk we were working hard to get ready for the coming season. It was going to be tough, because our school had just been placed in a new league. In the fall we were going to play a team that most considered the best in the area. Edison Consolidated was a big school that drew players from several communities, and I started thinking and planning about how we were going to win that game.

And I had an idea. I ordered jerseys.

I didn't mention it to the principal, Father Bodart, because he wouldn't probably have let me spend the money. So I didn't tell anybody what I had done. I stored the jerseys in boxes and kept them hidden in the locker room.

About an hour before our game with Edison, we put on our regular old jerseys to go out to the field to warm up. When we returned to the locker room, I pulled out the boxes of new jerseys and tossed the shirts around the room. The boys cheered excitedly, perhaps because the front of the jerseys said BEAT EDISON.

It was a bold move. I never gave much thought to what could have happened had we lost that game. I took a huge risk by ordering those jerseys and having the boys put them on. If we had lost that game, we'd have been the laughingstock of Ohio high school football.

But we played hard and won the game, 34–7.

Those jerseys didn't win the game, of course; the skill and talent of the boys did that. But the new jerseys did give them an edge and did give them confidence—and confidence gives you the edge in JS situations.

We had a great record at Norwalk. We lost one game in 1969, our first year. Father Bodart called me after the loss and said, "If you ever lose a game again, you will be leaving us." I think he was kidding, but I put my heart into that team. The next year we played ten and won ten, and the year after that we again won all our games. Then in the fourth year we played ten and lost one.

So I left.

But not because Father Bodart fired me! I left to take a position at Morehead State as a college coach, thus realizing a dream I'd had for a long time. Working at Norwalk had given me confidence. In my four years there, we went 38-2-0. That positive experience convinced me I could handle college football—the one thing I'd wanted to do nearly all my life.

I returned to my alma mater, Morehead State, as assistant football coach and defensive secondary coach. I knew I would be a good college coach, and Head Coach Jake Hallum gave me my first chance to prove it. We had a good season that year, going 7-3. But a few things off the field made that year difficult for Mickey and me.

While at Morehead, we had our second daughter, Marcy. Both of my girls are God's sweet gift to Mickey and me, but Marcy's birth was one of the darkest moments I have ever experienced. I'd call it a *defining moment,* a period when God allows changes in our lives that will challenge and build us up as His children.

I had already experienced a defining moment in my life: the night my dad died. And I would experience other defining moments after that first year at Morehead. But that year, Mickey and I almost lost Marcy—and I almost lost Mickey.

Football coaches work eighteen hours a day during the season, and even in the off-season they work long hours. On March 7, 1972, a pregnant Mickey called me at the office, crying. Gosh, she never cried. She's as strong a person as you'll ever meet. But she called that day, weeping.

Something was wrong with the baby.

I rushed home, called the ambulance, and we took her to the doctor, who was waiting for us at the curb. I knew it had to be serious! She took one look at Mickey and said, "I've called ahead. You need to take her right to the hospital."

We rushed Mickey to the hospital, where staffers were also waiting for us outside—never a good sign. They whisked her out of the ambulance (really, little more than a station wagon) and wheeled her into the hospital. I had no idea what was about to happen. I made my way to the waiting room and sat down.

Five minutes later, the doctor appeared and delivered the awful news. "Mike, here's the story. Your baby is dead and your wife has a fifty-fifty chance of making it."

The news stunned me. In shock, I just started praying and thinking, *I hope this is not gonna happen*. It was the lowest time in my life, other than when my dad died. I prayed hard, then had to wait some more.

Half an hour went by. Another half hour. Another hour. Two hours later, the doctor reappeared.

"We have a baby," he said. "The baby's alive, but she's in trouble. It looks like your wife will make it, so long as she doesn't get pneumonia. But you and the baby have to go to Lexington, Kentucky. There's something seriously wrong with the baby—she may have been cut off from oxygen—and I can't help her here."

So I took baby Marcy in the station wagon ambulance to Lexington, Kentucky. I stayed for three days with her, driving home an hour and a half each night to visit Mickey. Then the next morning I'd head west to Lexington once more.

The first night I sat in our living room and asked God some hard questions: "Why? Why now? Why is this happening?" I had said those very words once before, after I lost my dad.

And suddenly the verse that Sister Kathleen had explained to me back in sixth grade came into my mind again: "I know the plans I have for you; plans to prosper you and not to harm you; plans for a hope and a future." I had to trust the Lord that night that His plans for me—and for my wife and new daughter—were still in force, still under His control.

After two weeks in Lexington, Marcy came home from the hospital. She is a special child, God's gracious gift to us. She has to take a lot of medicines and still has seizures. But as I think about all the football players I have known, all the sports figures I've been privileged to meet, my biggest hero and the one person I consider most courageous is Marcy. She won't ever be the president of the United States. She may never marry. She will probably live with us all her life. But when I've been away on a speaking engagement, or on an ESPN game, and I get home at 2 a.m., Marcy's waiting for me with a hug. She's a loving child and she loves life.

God's plan was to bless me with two wonderful daughters, while I had prayed for sons—I admit it. I wanted a son in the worst way. I prayed that God would let me have a son for all the obvious reasons: sports, football, all the typical father-and-son things.

God gave me a "no" on sons, but a wonderful "yes" on what He knew would be best for me. This was only one case of many where I prayed hard for something, and God gave me an answer better than anything I could have imagined. My girls brought a distinct joy into my life, and every day they prove the truth of Jeremiah 29:11. God does know His plans for us, and they are for good. Mickey and I made it through because we held on to God's promise for our future.

That future, though, did not include Morehead. The next year, the university hired Roy Terry as head coach. The president, still Dr. Doran, brought me into his office and said, "Now, Mike, you know I want you to stay. But we've hired another coach."

Immediately I replied, "Dr. Doran, if I ever get a head coaching job, I don't want somebody telling me who's gonna stay and work with me. The head coach needs to pick his own staff. So, if it's all right, I'm gonna have to think about it."

It wasn't an easy decision. I loved Morehead and wanted to be loyal to it. But I got a call to interview at Struthers High School in Youngstown, Ohio. The district superintendent, Clyde Quinby, was a really good man. While I wanted to work for him, I also loved my alma mater. I felt really torn. Should I stay? Or should I go back to high school as a head coach?

When the folks at Morehead came back to talk to me again,

I decided to stay. So I called Superintendent Quinby to tell him of my decision.

"Clyde," I said, "I've decided not to come. I'm gonna stay in Morehead."

Clyde was understanding and said in a nice way, "Mike, if there's ever anything I can do for you, please let me know." I believed he meant it—and instantly I had grave doubts about my decision.

When I got off the phone, I told Mickey, "I really feel bad that I let this guy down. This guy's so *nice*."

I kept thinking and praying about the decision overnight. In the morning, I had changed my mind. I called Clyde back and told him I was coming.

Later I told Clyde how I had agonized over the decision and how his phone call had made the difference. Clyde just smiled and said, "I use that trick on a lot of people. It always works."

So we moved on to Struthers High School in Youngstown, Ohio. A high school coach is more of a central figure than a college coach, because he sees the players more, both in classes and other activities throughout the year. That's why I think every coach should work at a high school at least once. I was there for two seasons, but God had yet more changes in store.

Dave Pavlansky, a good coach at another high school in Youngstown, called me one night and said, "Mike, I need to get with you. Something's come up that I need you to help me with."

I met Dave at a little restaurant. "I have a chance to go with Rey Dempsey," he explained. "He's gonna hire one high school coach."

"That's great," I said.

"Can I ask you why you left Morehead?" Dave was curious about college coaching.

"I left Morehead because I didn't know the new coach coming in. He's a nice guy, but he didn't know me and he was bringing in his own guys. So I figured I should leave."

Dave nodded. "Tell me about working there, at the college level. What about the time away? Did you have to spend a lot of time away from your home?"

"It is different from high school, because as a college coach, you're recruiting, you're doing scouting, and you're working longer hours. You do have to be away."

"Well, I have six kids," Dave said—and I think he had one more on the way.

I saw where his mind was taking him. "No, Dave, I think you'll like it. Youngstown's a good place." I encouraged him to take the job, but I could tell he was worried about whether he wanted to be away from his family as much as the job might require.

Dave eventually turned down the offer—and about a week later, Rey called to see if I'd be interested. Rocky Alt, who worked with me at Struthers, was close to Rey, and that's how Rey learned about me. I've always looked up to Rey Dempsey. He's been a mentor to me most of my career.

"Mike," Rey said, "I have an opening at Youngstown, offensive coordinator. Would you be interested?"

I was ready again for college ball. I even took a pay cut to work at Youngstown. Clyde Quinby was the main reason I'd taken the job at Struthers, and he was leaving for Naples, Florida. I figured that made it a good time for me to leave, too. God's plans at work once again!

We continued to live in Struthers while I coached at Youngstown. We had a big year, going 8-2. Rey taught me a proper work ethic and how to be a student of the game and of the opponent. I learned how to bring authority and toughness to the team in a respectful and caring way.

I would have stayed at Youngstown a lot longer with Rey, but when he left for the Detroit Lions, once again it was time to move. That's just how coaching goes—you have to keep moving.

I had always talked about Cincinnati and working for Tony Mason. Tony was a great coach and a popular banquet speaker. I'd heard him speak around the country, and so far as I was concerned, he was the best speaker out there. I followed his progress and had thought many times, *Someday I'd like to work for Tony Mason.*

Then one day Tony called me and said, "Mike, I'm working on something for you right now. I'd really like you to work with me." Although Mickey and I felt excited about the possibility, we couldn't tell anybody at Youngstown because we didn't yet have the job.

But inside our family we talked about it. We told the girls,

"We're gonna move close to Kings Island, the amusement park, and you're gonna have so much fun!" We were preparing them for another move.

After Rey left Youngstown, Bill Narduzzi took over. Bill wanted to get to know me and my family, so we had him over for dinner. We were all sitting at the table and he looked at my daughter and said, "Mindy, we're gonna have a good team in Youngstown next year." Bill was trying hard to get me to stay. "I have six kids and you're gonna join my family."

Mindy didn't miss a beat. "I'm not gonna be at Youngstown," she declared. "I'm gonna be at Kings Island near Cincinnati."

Mickey and I looked at each other, and then at Bill. Fortunately, he didn't seem to grasp the meaning of Mindy's comment and we quickly tried to pull out of the dilemma. "Could you pass the spaghetti?" I asked, as Mickey said, "Mindy's always dreamed about going to Kings Island."

The social faux pas thus averted, someone passed the spaghetti and the conversation moved to another topic. But much to the delight of both Marcy and Mindy, Kings Island really was the next stop on our God-ordained itinerary.

FILL THE GAP

Without question, a dad should have fun with his kids. He should play with them and laugh with them. But when a father tries to be a boy and attempts to act like a kid instead of an adult, it just doesn't work. A dad needs to maintain some separation—a separation of authority. A dad needs to be in charge of his family, just as a coach is in charge of his team. No questions.

A man's family feels a sense of security when everyone knows he's taking responsibility. It gives them confidence and helps with their fears. They can sleep better when they know someone who cares about them is willing to take on the authority role. This isn't a gender or man-versus-woman issue; it's just a matter of someone being in charge.

Every boy needs to learn the lessons of authority that a dad is divinely charged to give. So when a boy doesn't have a dad, he needs to learn those lessons from someone else. At Team Focus, we try to fill some of that gap.

As we walked down the street at San Diego State University, heading for the cafeteria, our group of boys—fifty-two strong—filled more than a block of sidewalk. They wore the T-Shirt color of the day, gray with the Team Focus logo. The boys, ranging in age from nine to seventeen, were laughing, talking about the earlier softball game, and mixing it up with their adult counselors and mentors.

Just then two good-looking girls from the university walked

by on the right. From somewhere in the center of this river of testosterone came the sound of whistles, understated hoots, and catcalls—nothing too unexpected from a group of adolescent males.

But that's when Pastor Stuart Parham halted the parade up short.

"Stop right here," he said. "You can't talk to a girl like that and call yourself a man!" He gathered a group of about a dozen boys who seemed to be near the general source of the hooting. "If you want to be a real man, you better learn how to treat a woman with respect, and catcalls don't show respect."

A hand went up in the front of the group. A smallish ten-year-old asked, "What's a catcall?" It wasn't a joke; he really didn't know.

Stuart looked down at the boy. "Josh, you come talk to me about that later."

Pastor Parham is from the Watts subdivision in Los Angeles, but long before that, he played football for me at Kansas as defensive tailback from 1983 to 1986. In this streetside moment at our last San Diego camp, Stuart drew a line and set a boundary to establish authority.

The impromptu lecture lasted a few more minutes. Stuart combined respect with strong words in his rebuke. Then, with a gentle smile aimed at his boys, he said, "Now, boys, let's go get some lunch," and the parade marched on to the cafeteria. That moment is what a Team Focus camp is about.

All of us are prone to buck authority, but having someone in charge who is good at it provides security. If I have a boss at work that I trust, who cares not only about making money but also about me and my life, his authority over me feels both safe and valuable. God, who loves us and cares about every detail of our lives, exercises His authority, not to make us angry and rebellious, but to provide for us a secure existence. Godly authority gives us boundaries of behavior that protect us from our own failings and proneness to sin.

We don't make apologies for the boundaries we set at Camp Focus. We tell the boys not to bring earrings, bracelets, necklaces, cell phones, video games, CD players, or iPods, and we cut the TVs in every room. It's not because we want to be tough; it's because we want them to interact with real, live people. Camp is five long days, but they can handle it. The boys sign a contract that they won't use that stuff while they're at camp. It's a boundary.

A camp counselor once came to me with a sheet of paper covered with signatures. "I don't want to do this," he said apologetically, "but I have to do it. I have to give you this resolution." He handed me a piece of paper with a statement and lots of names.

"I know the rules, and I signed that I would keep them," he said. "All the guys up in our room signed, too. I understand why we need them. But we'd like to have our TV on for one hour." They wanted to watch a show and had written up their request formally. Even a counselor had signed it. But I stuck to my guns.

"Good try," I said, "but it's not up for negotiation."

This was not rules for rules' sake, but a lesson in authority and training for the real world.

Part of growing up is experiencing loving authority without resentment. Loving authority is not capricious, so we tell the boys and their moms up front about our expectations. We get them up at 7 a.m. and don't stop until 11 p.m. We insist that the guys take notes during lectures—and there are hours of lectures every day. Devotions with a pastor in the morning and worship before bed are not optional. Being a part of Team Focus is a responsibility, an investment we ask the boys to make. Camp is not for everybody.

So we tell them, "Here are the rules. Here's what you'll be doing and here is how the camp will be." Some boys don't make it and we've had to send a few home.

The boys who come to Team Focus often have moms who struggle with grief, guilt, stress, and exhaustion. It's no wonder that they sometimes struggle with authority.

A dad in the home provides the sense that someone is in charge, someone is taking care of things, someone has authority. Dads provide a source of strength and some muscle behind the decisions boys make every day. Without that muscle, it's easy to make the wrong decisions. Boys can't do it alone; the statistics prove it over and over. We can't discipline boys in Team Focus the way a father would, but we can help them with boundary issues they will face every day.

How? For one thing, we talk to the boys about peer pressure and offer the advice and the confidence that enables a boy to buck the crowd. These boys need a father-figure in their lives to be a watchman. They need men around them who will take the challenge to fill that gap by showing authority. If they have no father to say, "No, I don't want you to do that," or, "Yes, that's a great thing to do," then someone's got to step in. So I decided when we started this thing that I would not only show loving authority at camp, but step up to the plate where the boys live.

In 2002, Rocky Alt and I (at the time our Team Focus director in Michigan) walked into a grade school in Detroit to meet with the principal. We had been called in to help out with the Landon twins, Greg and Ted, eighth-graders who had attended our Camp Focus in Ann Arbor.

"These guys need your help," the principal explained. "They need to work harder in school. They're not bad boys, but their grades need to improve. They could be doing much more. I know they've been through a lot, but I don't want them to fall behind."

Christy, our guidance counselor with Team Focus, keeps track of the boys and their academic progress. She maintains contact with their teachers, counselors, and administrators at schools across the country. When a boy is involved with Team Focus, the school knows about us and will often give us a call. I've told the boys that I could show up at any time at their school, and I've been called in to help with struggling kids.

I offered the principal anything I could do to help. "Okay," I said, "let me start by talking to them. I'll get them going."

"I'll go down to the class and get them," she said, then left to fetch the Landon brothers. While Rocky and I waited, we walked out in the hall. I looked down the corridor to see the principal escorting the two boys—about four foot eight inches tall, skinny as rails—one on either side of her. And it just hit me. I turned to Rocky.

"You know, I spent all my life in schools, going to high schools on recruiting trips, visiting big quarterbacks and running backs and three-hundred-pound tackles. Now here I am, ready to meet with these two boys walking down the hall. But you know, Rocky, this is more important than getting that quarterback or getting that tackle. *Way* more important."

I sat the boys down in the office with all these things flashing through my mind. "The principal tells me you're not working hard enough and not getting your homework done," I said. "What do you say to that?"

They answered as one: "It's true, Coach. We're not doing it. We're not doing what we're supposed to do."

Even as they admitted the problem, I continued to think about how my life had changed. If I had pulled one of my football players into my office to talk about his lackluster grades, he'd always try to blame someone else. But here were the Landon twins owning up to their problems. It threw me back a little.

After we talked it out, they agreed to do better, Rocky stayed on top of them, and today they're in high school and doing great. I can't be their father, but I can offer the loving authority that comes in the general shape of a dad.

That's why I'm doing this. A father comes alongside a boy and guides him through tough choices. He helps him make the decisions that will lead him in a good direction. Where will that guidance come from if a boy doesn't have a dad who can provide an environment of security? I want to put myself into that family picture so that when a boy faces the crossroads between good and bad, he can have confidence enough to head in the right direction. I want to offer loving authority.

Randall is a good kid who lives with his mom and grandma. He's a sharp kid, an A student, but suddenly he started letting his grades drop. Randall's mom called me and told me what was going on. It wasn't the first time Randall had needed some help, and it wouldn't be the last, but it was my turn to deal with him. I shifted some plans with Mickey, arranged to meet with her later, and made an appointment with Randall.

We met at McDonald's for a Coke. I asked him what was happening at school, and he told me he just had a case of the blahs.

"Now, everybody gets the blahs," I said. "It happens to all of us once in a while. But you can't stay there. You have to get out of that." I took him by the collar and looked him in the eye. "Look around here. You could own a McDonald's, or you could work at one. What do you want to do? You're an A student, you can do anything you want to do. What are you going to choose?"

I was tough with him and let him know in no uncertain terms that I loved him and expected him to turn things around. I gave him some advice and told him I'd be tracking his progress. And then I took him shopping. After Randall picked out some new clothes, I took him to Bath & Body Works and had him pick out presents for his mom and grandma.

Later that day I took Randall with me to meet Mickey.

Randall showed off his big bag of clothes to Mickey, who watched as he reached back in the car for the Bath & Body Works bag. Then she looked at me. "What did you do?" she demanded.

"Well, I had a little talk with him."

Mickey pointed to the shopping bags. "So, *this* is what happens when Randall gets into some trouble?"

What could I say? I'm a little softhearted when it comes to these guys. But a soft heart with firm, loving discipline lays a foundation for security in a boy's life. And a boy without a dad needs someone to supply that authority.

Dear Team Focus,

The last twelve years have been hard for Greg and myself. At the time Greg's father died, he owed us $60,000 in back child support. It's been hard, but we've made it.

Greg and I fought about him going to Camp Focus. He finally said he'd go, and then I told him your rules: no cell phones, no CD players, no watching TV, etc. We fought for a few more days after that. He went to camp anyway.

When he called me on Saturday morning during camp, I was on my way out the door to my part-time job. He said I needed to come pick him up from camp because he'd been bad and they were kicking him out. I could have wrung his neck! But then he said, "Just kidding, Mom!" and he started telling me

what he'd been doing. He was talking a mile a
minute, so fast I could hardly understand what he
was saying. He was having an AWESOME time, he
said. I was so happy!

Thanks to all of you,

Cindy

CHAPTER SEVEN

REALIZING THE DREAM

During my early coaching days, three men joined the ranks of those who have most influenced me. God used this team of mentors to speak into my life and help fill the gap. They taught and modeled for me what a good coach looks like: Jake Hallum from Morehead, Rey Dempsey from Youngstown, and Tony Mason from Cincinnati.

All three believed in positive coaching and always "coached up." They cared about their players and encouraged and supported them. I got to work as an assistant with all three of these men, and each one taught me important lessons about how to coach at the collegiate level. I would not be where I am today except for these three coaches.

■

In 1975 Tony Mason hired me as the offensive backfield coach at Cincinnati. We had two winning years together and I learned a lot from Tony. When at the end of that time he moved to coach at the University of Arizona, I packed up the family and moved to Tucson along with him.

That's how it was usually done: an entire staff moved as a group. Even so, I wasn't sure I wanted to move to Tucson. Tony had called me during a recruiting trip to Crestline, and he said, "Mike, tomorrow I'll either be named the head coach of Miami or Tucson."

I hope it's Miami, I thought. *Please, Lord, let it be Miami.*

"By the time you get back to Cincinnati tomorrow morning," he continued, "I will have taken one of those two jobs—and I'm going to want you to go with me."

Arizona sounded like Afghanistan to me—hot, dry, desert. I'd never been that far west. I drove back to Cincinnati early the next morning, thinking all the way, *Things are about to change again.* When I got home, I called around and found out where I might be headed: Tucson.

Just great.

Every Christmas we had a party, and this time around Tony was in Arizona sealing the deal for his new position. He called the party and wanted to talk to each of us individually about what we were going to do. My turn came up.

"Okay, Mike, are you going to come?"

"I need to think about this, Tony. Tucson is a long way away from my family—my mom and Mickey's mom and dad. Let me think about this."

"Okay, Mike. But you don't have long."

I was the last guy on the staff to decide to go. I stalled because Cincinnati offered me a chance to stay. But I really loved Tony, and the only reason I didn't want to go was that Tucson seemed so far away. Mickey and everyone else on staff seemed excited about going, but I worried over my decision. I knew I would be recruiting a lot, so I'd still get to see my mom, but still it was a tough move.

We stayed in Arizona one year before God showed us the next step on our sojourn. Now it was time to test my wings.

I took my first head-coaching job at the college level in December 1977. We stayed at Murray State for three seasons.

Our rivalry team was Western Kentucky, and I knew going in that if I was going to have a successful career, I had to beat Western Kentucky more times than they beat me. It was the JS team to beat.

Once while driving through Bowling Green, home of Western Kentucky University, I decided to get off the freeway, drive through town, and visit the campus. I looked over the stadium and in my imagination pictured my Murray State team coming in here and winning the championship.

We lost to Western my first year at Murray. The second year, we beat them for the championship. But the third year they were coming to our campus, and we needed to win—even though they were the top-ranked team in the nation.

I knew we were going to win.

It's hard to explain, but I saw it before the game. Not all the individual plays or even a game plan, but I saw in my head a vision of a big win. A blowout, really, which was something, considering our chances. We were going into the game as a big underdog.

And we beat them soundly. We crushed the number one football team in the whole country, 49–0—and I had seen the whole game ahead of time. So even before the opening kickoff I was able to tell the boys, "Boys, we're going to win today." It makes a big difference if you know the outcome ahead of time!

I wish I could say all my games were like that, but they weren't, of course. In a similar way, not all God's plans for me have been revealed ahead of time, and many of the people I've met along the way had no place in my vision of what God had for me to do. But He planned for specific people to come bubbling up into my life at just the right time to get me ready for something I'd never dreamed.

Richard Ellison was his name, but everybody called him Speck.

When I took the job at Murray State, he was in school and had no one to back him up—no mother and no father that I knew of. He got bad grades and was losing his student status, so he had become the manager of our football team. The players loved him, the staff accepted him, and he became part of the family. When I arrived, he became my responsibility. The guy had no home, nowhere to go, no money, and no food.

I took an immediate liking to him.

The school gave us meal chips that allowed our players to take extra cafeteria trips, and I gave them to Speck. "Here, Speck," I'd say. "You've got a thousand dollars' worth of meal chips. So make sure you eat."

When I discovered he had nowhere to sleep, I moved him into the stadium. "Speck," I told him, "you can stay in the stadium. You can sleep here." Everybody said he lived in the biggest house in the county.

All in all, I'd say Speck had a pretty good life at Murray. Sooner or later, of course, I knew we would have to make other arrangements. Sure enough, when the administration found out he was living in the stadium, they told me, "He can't sleep in the stadium. If the place burns down, we'll get sued." So I searched for another place and got him into a dorm.

One day I got a call from a bill collector representing the phone company. "Mike," he said, "I'm on my way over there to interview three of your players. They owe us a lot of money." The incident happened right in the middle of the season, and I didn't need the interruption.

"Who are the players?" I asked.

"Greg Evans is one."

Now, Greg Evans was one of the best players I had. "How much does he owe?"

"Thirty-five dollars."

Well, that's no problem, I figured. "Who's the next guy?"

"Sonny Burnett."

Sonny was a wide receiver. "How much does he owe?"

"Seventy-four dollars."

Okay, I thought, *that's workable.*

"But this third guy, Coach, he's the one I'm really looking for."

"What's his name?"

"Richard Ellison." Ah, that was Speck.

"How much does he owe?"

"Two thousand seven hundred sixty-five dollars."

I felt faint. That was a huge amount of money in those days. Right away I yelled out for the culprit. "*Speck!* Speck, there's a guy from the phone company calling, and you're in some trouble." When he came running, I said, "*What* are you thinking? What have you been doing?"

He mumbled something. Obviously he didn't realize the kind of bills he'd been racking up by calling friends and family all over the country.

"Listen," I said, "you're in big trouble. I don't know what we can do here, but I'm gonna tell you how to handle this. You listen to this guy; you listen to everything he says. You apologize. You do whatever he tells you to do—and then we'll see what we can do."

When the collections guy came in, I had Evans and Burnett there to pay him the money they owed. Then he said, "Okay, where's Ellison?"

First, I wanted to explain about Speck: "Well, let me tell you a little bit about Ellison. "Look. He has no family. He has no money. I know he's messed this thing up pretty bad, but I think it would be important for you to keep his situation in mind."

"Well," the guy answered, "I'll just scare him. Then we'll work out some kind of payment plan."

"Okay, he really is a great kid."

I called for Speck. He was just a little guy, but when he came in and sat down, he looked even smaller. "Speck," I said, "this is the guy from the phone company."

Immediately the man started in on him. He was really tough. "You're gonna go to jail. You know how many guys your size and your age are gonna be in jail?" He threatened prison; he threatened lots of things. He went on like this for about ten minutes. I didn't pay much attention because I was trying to get some work done, planning for the game.

Finally I heard Speck say, "Excuse me, sir. Could you leave the room a minute?" It not only shocked the guy; it shocked me, too. "I need you to leave the room so I can talk to Coach Gottfried here."

The puzzled guy said, "Sure. Okay." He looked at me, I looked at him, and both of us were trying to figure out what was going on. When the guy walked out, Speck turned to me and said, "What do we have to do now?"

"What are *we* gonna do?" I asked "*We?*"

Between me, the phone company guy, and Speck, we worked out a payment plan.

Speck became my own personal manager, in a way. He worked hard and did whatever I asked. So although it was hard to leave him behind when I left Murray State, we kept in touch. In fact, he'd call me all the time.

When I left Cincinnati to take the head-coaching job at Kansas, he called me one day and said, "I just wanted to tell you, I'm coming to Kansas." Then he hung up, before I could say anything. He knew I would say, "You can't come to Kansas."

Speck took a bus and brought all his stuff with him, so I figured I had to find a place for him. Later when I announced I was heading to Pitt, he made clear his desired future. He came up and asked me, "Are you going to take me, Coach?"

"Yeah, of course I am, Speck." So I took him to Pittsburgh. By that time I was kind of responsible for him.

Whenever the team traveled, Speck would go, too. He came with us when we played at the University of Colorado. Before the game, just as we did before every contest, the team got together on the field for the Lord's Prayer.

Colorado's mascot is the buffalo. Before each game, they bring out a buffalo and run it around the field in a certain pattern. But on this day, the buffalo got loose. So there we were, all huddled up for prayer. Our captain started out, "Our Father who art in heaven—"

All of a sudden, we heard Speck shout, "Here comes the buffalo! Here comes the buffalo!" That's just the way it came out: "Our Father who art in heaven—*here comes the buffalo!*" If Speck hadn't warned us, the beast would have knocked us all into tomorrow. As it was, everybody safely dove out of the way.

The athletic director at Pitt used to see Speck all the time and could never figure him out—nobody could. So the AD told me, "You know, Mike, I think we ought to give him a job in the university. That way, you don't have to worry about him." It was really a classy move. It allowed Speck to get some benefits, and he still has that job.

These days we bring Speck down to Mobile every year to help with the GMAC Bowl. God brought Speck into my life as a way of teaching me the process of coming alongside someone and helping him with the gap in his life.

In my progression from high school to college assistant to head coach, I knew I had to keep moving up—and that meant moving around. I moved my family ten times in thirteen years. My family thought the U-Haul truck was the family car.

When I left Murray State to take a head-coaching position at Cincinnati, I took my daughter Mindy to the school for my final interview. It took place during Christmas break when my eleven-year-old was off from school.

Mindy is a great football fan; she understood everything even as a youngster. "Honey," I told her, "I'm going to take this new job, where the team has won only four games in the last four years. I'm excited about this, and I want you to be a part of it."

After I officially took the job and held a press conference, the athletic director handed me the schedule for the next year. "You might want to go back and watch some of these teams on television," he advised me. "They're playing in bowl games right now, and your team is going to play against them next year."

I told Mindy, "Let's go back to the hotel and watch these games. We'll see who your dad's going up against next year."

The first night it was the Fiesta Bowl: Penn State and Ohio State. "Honey," I said, "we're going to open up against Penn State in front of ninety thousand people. Joe Paterno is their great coach, and we're going to get to coach against him." I always said *we* instead of *I* because my family was an important part of everything I did. We were all in this together.

The next night in the Gator Bowl, South Carolina was playing Pittsburgh. "Honey," I said, "do you see that Pittsburgh team? We're going to play them after we play Penn State. We're going to play Pittsburgh in front of their home fans—sixty thousand screaming people. Their quarterback, Dan Marino, is one of the best. They have two good defensive ends, Ricky Jackson and Hugh Green, and I'm going to get to coach against that. And South Carolina will come after Pittsburgh."

The following night was the Orange Bowl, featuring Florida State and Oklahoma. "Honey," I said, "you see that Florida State team? We're going to go down to Tallahassee five straight years to play against them."

When Alabama came on in the Sugar Bowl, I went up to the TV and pointed at the image of Bear Bryant on the screen.

"Honey, you see that man? He's won more games in your dad's profession than any other man, ever. Your dad's going to take his Bearcat team down there to Alabama and play the Crimson Tide for their homecoming game, where they've won forty-eight straight games."

I turned around and saw Mindy crying. Instantly I thought, *Maybe I've made it sound too negative, too bad. Maybe she thinks it's a lost cause.*

I didn't know what had caused her tears, so I said, "It's going to be okay, honey. Daddy will be okay."

But that wasn't on her mind at all. Through her tears, Mindy asked, "Daddy—does this mean we have to move again?"

It did. We moved again.

I returned to Cincinnati as head football coach in 1981. In my first year we lost two games in a row, the first to Penn State (58–0) and then to Pitt (35–7). We practiced on Monday after the blowout.

As I watched the guys work out, it seemed as if no one on the field knew what he was doing. They just weren't working on the right things. I got frustrated, and as the team watched, I threw down my hat in anger. "You guys don't know how to practice!" I shouted.

One of our best players, Mike Gates, a senior and team captain, yanked off his helmet and threw it on the ground, right back at me. "Then *show* us how to practice, Coach!" he demanded. "We're tired of losing!" Everybody suddenly got quiet.

What he did stopped me in my tracks. In that moment, the significant men in my life came rushing back to my mind. Coach Hutson. Dr. Doran. Earl Bentley. Rey Dempsey. Tony. All of them. *Boy,* I thought, *those coaches would sure be disappointed in me now, the way I've reacted.*

So I determined to change. "Okay," I told my team, "we're gonna learn how to practice." I calmed everybody down and repeated it: "Okay. We're gonna learn to practice." And we got to work.

We turned it around that year, finishing with a good season at 6-5.

Wednesday night before we faced Alabama at its homecoming game, my team had a "players-only" meeting. Coaches know that a players-only meeting is not always a good thing, especially with a big game coming up against one of the best teams in the country. You never know what your guys are doing in there. One of my assistants came by and asked me, "Why are they having a players-only meeting?"

"I don't know," I answered. "I just hope they're going to go play the game. That's all I want—just play the game."

Sometime later a team captain knocked on my door. I let him in and he sat down. He looked nervous, almost as much as me, but I wasn't going to let him see it.

"Coach," he began, "we had a players-only meeting tonight."

"Yeah. I sort of heard about that." He waited for me to say something, ask a question or let him off the hook. I let him wait for a minute, then I asked, "So, what did you decide?"

"Well"—he hesitated—"we want you to know we love you, and you're our coach."

This is not good, I thought. "So, what is it?"

"Well, Coach, we'd like to get Bear Bryant's autograph before the game."

I secretly let out a big breath. "That's okay. You can get his autograph, so long as you play the game."

"Oh, we'll play. And we're gonna play hard, Coach."

That's all I needed to hear. Now I just had to figure out how one hundred guys were going to line up to get Bear Bryant's autograph.

Dr. Jake Smith from Morehead was at the game, down on the sideline. While I was talking to him before the kickoff, Speck came running up to me. "Coach, Bear Bryant's out in the middle of the field, looking for you."

"Okay, Speck, I'll be right out there," I replied, then turned to Dr. Smith.

He looked at me and said, "Son, it's time for you to go take your medicine!"

It was Bear Bryant's last homecoming game as the coach of the Crimson Tide, and 80,000 people filled that Tuscaloosa stadium—exactly 79,990 of whom were wearing red and crimson, pulling for Alabama. The other ten were wearing white, rooting for us—our wives.

The Tide had a great team that year, a great coaching staff, and one of the best head coaches ever. Our Cincinnati team was just the next in line of many teams to get beaten up by the Tide. But I felt good about the game and even thought we had a good chance to beat them. I always thought the same thing about every team I ever coached.

The referees were all from the Southeastern Conference—Alabama's conference. Toward the end of the first half, the score was still 0–0 when the Tide got the ball on the 30-yard line, going our way. We needed a turnover; we could use the short field for a quick touchdown.

Walter Lewis, the Tide quarterback, reversed and came down the line of scrimmage. Mike Gates, our captain, hit him in the shoulder pads and sternum as he pitched the ball. The ball hit the turf and started bouncing, real slow.

You know how, sometimes, things just slow down and you can see everything in slow motion? That's what happened at that moment. I saw the ball go down and I saw Mike Hurst, our other defensive end, get on top of the ball. So I started yelling.

"It's our ball! Our ball!" I shouted, and jumped and hollered and pointed in the direction of the goal. "It's our ball! It's our ball!" This was exactly what we needed.

But then I heard someone else yelling, just as loud and excited as me. "No! It's *our* ball! *Our* ball!" The voice came from one of the Southeastern Conference referees. "Run it this way!" He pointed in the opposite direction. "It's *our* ball!"

Right then, I knew we weren't going to win that game. It's tough enough to beat Bear Bryant on a normal day. It's *real* hard to beat him on his home field. It's *extremely* hard to beat him at homecoming, and nearly impossible at his last homecoming game.

They beat us 13–3 in a good game.

Both my years at Cincinnati we went 6-5. And then it was time to pick up and move again along the path God had planned.

From Cincinnati I went to Kansas, where I stayed three years. I really loved the AD at Kansas, Monte Johnson. He loved me and Mickey and our whole family. He even put it in the paper when he hired me. He told the reporter, "I love this guy!" In fact, he said it so often that the phrase kept popping up in the paper.

So one day I pulled him aside. "Monte, I know you're telling everyone you love me, but what happens if I lose?"

"Mike, if you lose, I'll still love you." He paused for a moment. "But I'll miss you."

That's why a coach's life is so nomadic. You have to pick up and leave whenever the timing is right.

I had a tough time at Kansas because the program was going into probation. When you're in a situation like that, you have to fight the buzz and coaching becomes a public relations job. We had a lot of critics, and when you're a leader, you can't answer them. Nor can you let them discourage you.

On our schedule that first year we had Northern Illinois, followed by Southern Cal, Florida State, and then the usual suspects in what was then the Big Eight: Oklahoma with Barry Switzer; Nebraska with Tom Osborne; Jimmy Johnson at Oklahoma State; Bill McCartney at Colorado. It was a tough schedule.

When you're in the locker room before a game, you know as you sit in there that you're going out to play an Oklahoma or a USC or a Nebraska. You know that as soon as you leave the locker room, you're going to hear eighty thousand people boo their heads off. You have a decision to make: it's faith or fear.

I never went into any game thinking I couldn't win. That's the decision I made every time, the decision to have faith.

We just *had* to win my first game as coach against Northern Illinois. The local newspaper announced to everybody, "Come and see this new coach. Let's give him one game to see what he can do." So the eyes of Kansas fans everywhere were glued on us.

With five seconds left to go in the game, the score was tied, 35–35. Northern Illinois lined up for a field goal to beat us. The kick drifted off to the right, so it appeared I had tied my first game.

But then I saw the penalty flag—offside, on us. The refs moved the ball five yards closer to the end zone, the guy kicked it right down the middle, and we lost, 38–35.

I ran out to the middle of the field to shake the hand of the opposing coach. That done, I ran for the locker room. *That game's over,* I thought. That's the way I always handled it; if you start to focus on the past, if you keep mulling it over and feeling bad about it, then you won't get ready for the next game. You have to forget it, learn from it, and get on to the next game.

But as I approached the entrance to the locker room, a loudmouthed drunk leaned over from the top of the stadium and yelled, "Gottfried, what are you going to do when you play a *real* team?" That's not verbatim what he said, of course. He cursed, which embarrassed me, because my wife, my kids, my coaching assistants, their wives, their kids, and the families of my players were all there. I got real mad—so mad my face turned red. I wanted to sprint to the top of the stands to strangle this drunken loudmouth and throw him off the edge. But I just let it go.

Besides, I was almost sure I recognized voice of the president of the University of Kansas up there.

That last part's a joke.

Joke or not, though, critics can climb all over you if you're not winning—and many times, even if you are. I worked hard with that team and got the Jayhawks to a 15-18-1 record in my three years there.

Everything I had experienced to that point prepared me for my most difficult job yet. And even with all that, I'm not sure I was ready for the next stop on the coaching train. It would be the last coaching job of my career, and it would test everything God had put me through and challenge the promise that He had given me a future and a hope.

FILL THE GAP

Inside their hearts, all boys are asking, *Am I a part of this group? Am I a part of you? Do you claim me as your own?* Being accepted gives a boy a positive identity. That's why one of the most crucial things a dad does is make his children feel they are loved and that they *belong*. It's not an ownership issue; it's a relationship issue.

For a boy to lose his dad, then, means that one of the mechanisms that helps him to feel part of the family is missing. And without the conviction of belonging, a boy can swim in a sea of self-doubt and fear. Sometimes boys drown and lose themselves in the anxiety of growing up. My prayer is that somehow I can step into the life of a boy and let him know he belongs.

Baldwin called me up one day and cried over the phone. "Coach," he said, "I have to resign my position at Team Focus." I started laughing to myself, because Baldwin didn't really have a "position" at Team Focus; he just loved us a lot. He takes it all seriously and is doing great.

"Baldwin," I replied, "what are you talking about? Why do you think you need to resign?"

He was still crying. "My mother told me that I have to resign because I didn't show integrity and I didn't show any leadership." He just sobbed.

"Well, try to stop crying and tell me what you did."

"I signed my mother's name on my report card and took it back to school, because I didn't want her to see it."

I'm glad he didn't see me smiling into phone. That Baldwin felt upset he might not be able to join us at Team Focus anymore meant that his involvement mattered to him, and that made me glad. I also felt happy to hear some genuine remorse in his voice over his misbehavior. It also pleased me that Baldwin and his mom had decided to call me, just as he might have called his father.

Baldwin Nelson is an eleven-year-old African-American who lives in Arkansas. I am white, but Baldwin tells people all the time that his last name is not Nelson, but Gottfried. During camp he will go up to perfect strangers, point to me, and say, "See that guy over there? He's my dad!" It's okay by me. I'm proud of Baldwin Gottfried—I mean, Nelson. Even when he messed up and forged his mother's signature, I considered him part of my family.

"Baldwin, let me tell you a story," I said. "One time I got an F on a report card. I didn't want my mom to see it, just like you. So I used a pencil and tried to turn the F into a B. And I got caught."

Baldwin stopped crying. "Really? You really did that, Coach?"

"Yeah, I did. That doesn't make what you did right, but it means that it happens to all of us sometimes. We do things wrong. But we admit it, we ask for forgiveness, and we learn not to do those same things again."

"Coach?" He was thinking through his options.

"Yeah, Baldwin?"

"Coach, would you tell my mama?"

I laughed out loud. "Put her on, Baldwin." And for a few minutes, Baldwin's mom and I talked about "our" boy.

Do you know what I was trying to accomplish when I told Baldwin about my grade-changing episode? I wanted him to know he was accepted, part of our crew, regardless of what he had done. Every boy needs to experience the power of acceptance, and that's a big part of what we try to provide at Team Focus.

And I know Baldwin benefits from knowing he's accepted! During one minicamp in Texas, a TV news crew asked Baldwin about his future. "I'm going to be a plastic surgeon," he replied. "I'm going to own my own private jet, and I'm going to fly all these people here over to Hawaii for a Team Focus camp."

Guys like Baldwin can change dramatically in five short days. Part of the reason for their accelerated growth is that they know we're all a team, a family—and that sense of being part of something is hard to come by in a home where Mom works all the time just to make ends meet and Dad's out of the picture. Team Focus is a second family, and a family is a place of acceptance. A place where you belong.

It costs the boys nothing to be a part of Team Focus. Everybody is welcome. For me, it comes down to this: Would a family make a kid pay for vacations? Would a dad charge his son for a fishing trip? Being accepted means that you are part of something, that you belong, and making a boy pay for his supper doesn't convey that idea at all.

While belonging means being accepted for who you are, I

believe that before you can really know acceptance, you must come clean about the truth. One of the things the boys get at Camp Focus is the truth. We tell them the truth about our lives, about what it's like to be without a dad. We don't spend all week talking about it, but we carve out specific time to let men and boys tell their stories.

These boys tend to lock everything inside them. No one feels eager to talk about the death of his dad, and in typical circumstances it is hard to find a safe place to do so, even if you do want to talk about it. Moms often don't want to talk about it because the father's death still fills them with enormous pain, and they feel a need to "be strong for the kids." Boys can't talk to other boys about it because they have to keep face, keep tough. And girls are just out of the running. So boys learn to bury it, to lock it up so it doesn't come out.

In some of our boys, this deep hurt has never seen the light of day—but if it's not dealt with, it festers and seeps out in inappropriate ways. I've encountered guys who go through their days with a blank stare on their face, a look that betrays the emptiness inside. Our goal is to talk with the boys until they get it out of their system.

Davis was working for us one summer at a Team Focus camp in Washington, D.C. At an evening session I was sharing some thoughts with the boys, and I began to tell Davis's story. I'd forgotten that Davis was right there, and I began telling how his mother had died after asking Mickey and me to take care of her son. From somewhere in the auditorium, I heard crying.

Now, crying is not unusual. The boys have moments when they let down their guard, because it's safe to do so at camp. But this crying clearly came from a deep place; someone was sobbing uncontrollably. Mickey looked around while I tried to determine where those sobs came from.

It was Davis. Davis wasn't new to any of this. He'd been with us for about six years and had been through all of it before. But this was the first time he had let out the emotion. Davis was a tough guy; he didn't want to show the pain. But at that moment the dam broke and he just let it all go.

About two years ago a woman from Texas brought her nephew to Team Focus. Gregory had witnessed his dad shoot and kill his mom, then point the gun to his own head and kill himself. Gregory had grown up hearing shotgun blasts every night in his neighborhood. His aunt didn't know if he'd be able to spend even one night at the camp; it frightened him to be alone.

Gregory was all locked up, full of pent-up anger. So I talked to him whenever I could, and the camp counselors also kept talking to him, telling him about our own lives. Eventually, Gregory learned we were in this thing with him. We were all family and it was safe to talk about the pain of the past. At Team Focus he found a place where he was accepted, where he belonged. He's doing great these days and is excited about life.

Most of the men helping in the program have suffered the loss (or profound absence) of their own father, and they often let the emotion of their experience come out during camp. Because they are honest enough to tell their stories and brave enough to let some tears roll down their cheeks, the boys come to know that it's all right to admit the truth, that not having a dad really hurts. When we feel accepted, we can tell our own stories. And when we tell our stories and let out the emotion, the walls come down and the masks come off.

Latrell wore a mask from the very beginning. He came into camp with a bad attitude, ready to buck the system and work hard not to have a good time. It was all a mask, all self-protection. I told him to let it go, to take off the mask. But he wasn't listening and the mask stayed on. He got into trouble early on and I threatened to send him home. One of the counselors pulled me aside and said, "Let me try talking to Latrell first."

"No," I insisted, "he's done here. He's not going to make it." I knew that sometimes it just doesn't work out.

But the counselor persisted. He approached Latrell and said, "Look, you're going to be heading home and out of this program unless something changes. I want you to stay. I think you can do this and I'm going to stake my reputation on it. If you don't come through, I'm never going to be able to get a guy into this camp again."

Latrell stayed, he apologized, and the mask came off—not all at once, of course. But by the end of camp, Latrell had gained enough courage to share his story with his newfound family. How could he do it? Because he knew he belonged. He knew he was accepted. Latrell discovered a second family, and today he is free of his mask of self-protection.

Latrell has been with us now for five years. He is a nice

young man who calls me all the time. He has more self-confidence and is getting good grades in high school. One of our pastors says, "You might not look at Latrell and say, 'There's college material.' And I don't know if he'll go or not. But he's alive today, four years after he saw his cousin murdered. He's alive today, and Team Focus has a lot to do with that."

The old King James Version of the Bible translates a phrase in Ephesians 1:6 as "accepted in the Beloved," referring to our identity in Christ. Let me tell you, it's one thing for us to "accept" Jesus as Lord and Savior. But it is beyond amazing to consider that *He accepted us* in His love! We belong to Him, we're part of His team, His family. We've been accepted.

We want to pass that same sense of belonging on to boys without fathers, boys who need a flesh-and-blood way to know acceptance.

When I arrived at this camp I was a person with bottled-up emotions. My father had lost his battle with colon cancer the year before. I was in much pain and was negative about everything, believing that no good could come from this camp or anything else.

But by the end of the second camp I did something I never saw myself doing. I stood up before the whole camp and shared my story with the other boys who were there. I had barely been able to utter a word about my loss before that day; I didn't think

it would help to verbalize my feelings of my life experience. I let out my bottled-up emotions over two
years after my father's passing. It felt good, I felt a
heavy weight lift off my heart, and I became a lighter
person and understood the purpose of Team Focus.
Thank you, Team Focus, for the wisdom, for it has
truly changed my life in so many ways.

Stephen

CHAPTER EIGHT

HIGHS AND LOWS
IN THE PITT

The football program at the University of Pittsburgh had been experiencing some real problems.

And then they hired me.

Before the hard times, the school had enjoyed a history of winning. Johnny Majors coached Pitt in the late seventies and won a national championship. Jackie Sherrill followed with several winning seasons and plenty of bowl games. Foge Fazio then took over. He won for a couple of years, then lost one year, and then lost a second year—and they fired him.

That's when I came in.

From the beginning, I could see signs of trouble. During my interviews, Mickey, Mindy, and I had dinner one night with a few of my future coworkers. We observed them drink a lot, become inebriated, then start discussing changes in the details of my contract—details on which we'd agreed earlier in the day. It was clearly not a stable environment and not what I was used to.

I would revisit that scene many times while at the university.

Back in the hotel room I said to Mickey, "It looks like we're going to be dealing with some people here at Pitt that are a little different. I'm not so sure about this. I'm not sure we're supposed to be here. We'll see." But I signed the contract anyway and came to Pitt.

Nobody wants to be the father of losers, and I had come to a bunch of people who all blamed each other for the losing streak. Infighting was constant, and I got thrown into the center of it. The players blamed the coaches, the coaches blamed the administrators, the administrators blamed the players, and everyone had their finger pointed at everyone else. Nobody thought it was his problem or that he had contributed anything to it. There was no "team" attitude. Everyone was playing a big-time blame game. Add to that an athletic director who didn't like some of the boosters (and boosters who didn't like him), and you had all the makings of a huge mess.

And here I was, in the middle of it all. I had to make sense of it and somehow turn the program around.

I left most of the adults to fight it out and chose to start with my players. I had good recruiters, the best staff, and good support from the athletic department, but those things alone can't make a team successful. So I concentrated on my players.

First, I came in tough. Losing promotes selfishness, and you have to drive that disease out of a program. You can always ease up later on, but you can never really toughen up if you come in easy. I decided I wasn't going to take anything; I wouldn't put up with horseplay. I wouldn't give my guys a lot of wiggle room, at least not at first. It was like being a new teacher in a rowdy classroom—you have to hang tough.

But I also wanted my players to know I was on their side. In the big college leagues, physical touch becomes more important than ever. I'd say it's crucial if you want to show your guys affection. As a head coach, you don't get to spend the kind of time with each player that a coordinator does, so when the team did warm-ups on the field, I'd get out among the players and touch a guy on his shoulder or slap him on his helmet. I'd stop and put my arms around a guy to see how he was doing.

Next, I emphasized what we were doing right. You can't get anywhere with a team if all you ever do is harp on the negatives. Most of the time, players already know when they're blowing it. So I learned to focus on strengths. The average football game has over one hundred plays, so if we did poorly on eighty or ninety plays, but had success with fourteen plays, I'd say, "Okay. Look at these fourteen plays. These were great plays. If we can put together a whole game of these fourteen plays, we'll win every time!"

Recruiting is one of the biggest elements in a successful college program, and I've done a lot of it. At Pitt, we had re-cruiters who scouted prospective players, but I visited the best prospects myself. This one-on-one attention sometimes became the deciding factor in getting a player to come to Pitt. I told my recruits, "Look—all the schools chasing you are probably going to offer you a scholarship, and that's good. You'll be able to get a good education at any of them. But what I have to offer goes beyond the scholarship. I'm offering you a staff that will pay attention to you. They will care about you and get involved with you and will help you any way they can to make sure you succeed." I always figured that when I offered a scholarship, I was offering a piece of myself at the same time.

While at Kansas I recruited Danny Crossman as a defensive back. He didn't have a dad, so I gravitated toward that need in his life and paid close attention to him. When I decided to leave for Pitt, Danny told me he wanted to go with me. After getting permission from Bob Valesente, my replacement at Kansas, Danny transferred to Pitt. He sat out his sophomore year and lost his position as defensive back to another of my recruits, Louis Reddick. But Danny played the next year, starting eleven games at fullback as a junior and rushing for 273 yards and two touchdowns. As a senior, Danny had sixty-two tackles and one interception playing the strong-safety position and was named team MVP.

Today Danny is head special-teams coach for the NFL's Carolina Panthers. I can't take credit for Danny's success, but I can tell you that when you pay attention to your players, giving them time and energy, you build your team.

Most of all, to make a football program work, the people involved have to learn to function as a family. I set out at Pitt to make sure everyone knew he was an important part of the team.

Nobody showed up at the offices on Sunday. After preparing all week for a game on Saturday, Sunday was the one day that most everyone used to rest. One Sunday I went into the office at around 9 a.m., a rare occurrence for me. I was surprised to see Keith Howard and Tim Washington, our team managers, cleaning up the equipment to get things ready for the following week. After a while I said, "You guys want to get some lunch?"

"No thanks, Coach," they replied. "We don't eat lunch," explaining that they didn't have money for it. Immediately I ordered them some pizza, because I knew they were working hard for the team. They were an important part of the Pitt football family, and I wanted them to know it. From that time on, I had a standing order for a pizza to be delivered every Sunday to the locker room.

Keith Howard is now a football coach at Crossland High School in Upper Marlboro, Maryland. He also heads up our Washington, D.C., Team Focus operation.

Another critical principle that helped us succeed at Pitt was knowing the enemy. I knew that if we were going to win, I would have to find out everything I could about our opponent. I had to know what I was up against.

In fact, I wanted everyone on my staff to find out what the opponent was doing. I got with the strength coach and said, "Find out everything about their strength program." I found the academic guy and said, "Find out everything they send in the mail to recruits about their academics." I told the offensive guys, "You study their defense, so that you know their defense better than they know it." I had defensive guys studying the offense. Even the special teams coaches had their study assignments.

I soon got interested in hiring a guy for a special teams job. Scott O'Brien is now with the Dolphins, but in those days, college teams didn't have special-teams coordinators; the other coaches just shared the task. But I thought, *If it's good enough for pro, it's good enough for Pitt.* So I met Scott in Las Vegas for an interview and asked him to come out to Pittsburgh for a visit.

When Scott arrived at Pitt, I said to him, "I want you to go upstairs and watch all the Penn State tapes, and then come down and give me a game plan." I figured if he could come up with a good game plan, I would hire him. If he couldn't, I'd send him on his way. Scott studied the tapes and came down with a *great* game plan. I hired him, based on what he discovered about Penn State—because we had to beat Penn State, our biggest rival. And to beat them, we first had to understand them.

In 1986, my first year at Pitt, we had a break-even season at 5-5-1. But we did accomplish one major goal, a high point for any Pitt football team. We beat Notre Dame *at* Notre Dame.

October 11, the third game of the season, we confronted the Fighting Irish in their own stadium in front of their loyal,

die-hard fans. Among them were a contingent of my friends
from Crestline and Norwalk. This game garnered great interest
among my friends, not only because I was coaching Pitt, but
because I was going up against the Catholic college to which all
of my friends had a close connection and loyalty. I may have
had more people on the sidelines at that game than at any other
time in my career—even though I can't say they were all rooting for my team! That's part of why it was such a thrill when
Pitt defeated Notre Dame, 10–9, on a last-minute field goal by
Jeff VanHorne (Notre Dame's "Touchdown Jesus" notwith-
standing).

John Dipietro, my buddy from Crestline, visited the locker
room after the game. Now, John is a lifelong Notre Dame fan,
or should I say, *fanatic*. When you ring the doorbell at John's
house, it plays the Notre Dame fight song. His car's license
plates advertise his love for the team. John approached me and
took my hand in his two hands. "Good game," he said, but he
couldn't look me in the face. As he looked away, I saw a hint of
a tear in his eye. He congratulated me, despite his deep hurt
that his beloved Fighting Irish had lost.

Some of the most memorable games of my career took
place at Pitt. In November of 1986 at Pitt Stadium, Craig
"Ironhead" Heyward rushed for 254 yards in a loss to Miami.
The next year, the Pitt Panthers upset previously undefeated
Notre Dame, 30–27, in a nationally televised game, this time at
home in front of our fans. That year, Pitt also played Temple
under the lights, the first night game using permanent lighting
at Pitt Stadium.

My second year at Pitt, we won eight games and lost three. We beat Notre Dame, whipped Penn State, and went to the Blue Bonnet Bowl against Texas. Unfortunately, we lost that game to the Longhorns by a score of 31–27, ending the season with a record of 8-4. The third year we had another winning season, beating Penn State and BYU and finishing the season at 6-5.

Our second game of that third season, we played Ohio State at Panther Stadium. The week before the big game, my whole team watched the Buckeyes play Syracuse. As I watched the television, I just knew we could beat Ohio State. I knew this would be a big game for us, and a lot of my staff and most of my closest friends were from Ohio; I knew many would be in the stands that day.

When I came out onto the field on game day, I saw red everywhere. I went to shake hands with Ohio State's coach, John Cooper, and said, "I think you guys have as many fans in this stadium as we do—I've never seen so much red!" I didn't tell him we were going to win.

We beat the Buckeyes 42–10.

In 1989, we pulled a 7-3-1 season. We lost to Miami, which was ranked number one in the country; to Notre Dame, which was number two; and to Penn State, which was ranked number sixteen.

Four years and four winning seasons—that part of my experience at Pitt was good, *really* good.

You can see by now that I like to win. If you are a coach and you don't like to win, then you're in the wrong business. As I said, I never went into a game—not one—thinking that we had no option but to lose. Still, winning has never been the most important thing for me, and maybe that's what got me into trouble at Pitt. I wanted to win, but even more I wanted my players to get ahead in life. Paying attention to my players also got me in some trouble with pro teams, slimy agents, and even the mob. I never anticipated any of that.

During that era NFL agents started coming onto campus, recruiting and signing young guys and encouraging them to give up their scholarships and leave college. It was a controversial thing back then, and the debate still rages today.

I wanted my guys to graduate; in fact, I felt it was my responsibility as a coach. They had scholarships that made it possible for them to get a good education at a great school. If I thought they could make it all the way and get a degree, I wanted them to do it. Only a few of them were going to be stars in the NFL.

On the other hand, if the players were good enough to be first-round picks, then they were going to be okay. I felt genuinely happy for players if I believed they had a solid career ahead of them. But if they were down on the list and didn't make a pro team, not graduating from college would hurt them later on.

I don't deny it; I'd be crazy to say I had no interest in keeping good players. It is absolutely true that Pitt and other big college-football programs had a lot to lose if outstanding players left early to sign with the pros. But besides all that, the NCAA had strict rules about eligibility and how recruiting had to be done, and unscrupulous agents were blasting those rules to smithereens. So I took on the agents.

At the Blue-Gray game in 1986, I got invited to coach the all-stars for the Blue team, along with Rich Brooks from Oregon. What I saw there convinced me it was time to get involved and end the abuse. Agents seemed to be everywhere, buying expensive gifts for these kids, even using girls to bribe them—basically throwing money around in a blatant attempt to impress the players. It must have worked: I think they signed just about every player at the game. The abuse needed to stop, so I jumped in to see what I could do.

I made headlines by calling the agents buzzards, and I followed that up by offering my apologies to the buzzards for comparing them to agents. It wasn't that there were no good agents; there were. And at times I thought it was best for a certain player to pursue a pro contract. But the bad agents more than made up for all the good ones.

At the same time, Chris Mortensen, a reporter from the *Atlanta Journal-Constitution*, was researching and writing about the whole mess. He said agents had signed guys from Penn State, Notre Dame, Ohio State, all over. He also wrote about how the FBI was investigating agents and their possible ties to the Mafia.

One day Mortensen called me and told me that three of my guys had signed early because they were paid off. That was the last straw. "Chris, no, you're kidding me," I protested. "They wouldn't do that."

"No, it's true, Coach," he insisted. "You've got an agent problem at Pitt."

I couldn't believe it, but I had to do something.

I talked to the athletic director and the assistant AD, and we started looking into it. The last thing I wanted was to be accused of cheating. I called the FBI agent in charge of the investigation and he met me in my office.

"I can't tell you specifics about our investigation, Coach," he said, "but here's what you do. Go to the T-Check just off campus. It's a one-room operation. I don't know if it's true that your players are being bought or not, but you can start there. This is the last thing I'm going to say to you. I'm not telling you anything more." It was all very cloak-and-dagger stuff.

With the tip-off from the FBI agent, I took the assistant AD with me and drove over to the check-cashing joint. He stayed in the car while I went in alone.

I introduced myself to a man behind the counter, a short guy with a mustache. "I'm Coach Gottfried from the University of Pittsburgh," I announced. "I'm the football coach there, and I'm concerned that some of my guys are taking money from shady agents. I want to see your records of checks cashed. I want to see if my guys are in on it."

"I can't do that," the little man said. "You need to leave. *Now.*"

"Look, I gotta see what's going on here. Just let me have a look."

"You need to leave."

"You know, I can bring the FBI in here. They're gonna search your records, anyway. If I leave now, I'll be back and I'll bring them with me, and we'll get those records."

When I mentioned the FBI, the man with the mustache got real worried.

"Okay. Look," he said. "I'm going to step into my office back there. I'm going to leave some papers on my desk, and then I'm going to walk out of the office. When I leave the office, you might go in there and look at those papers, but I didn't tell you to do it, and I didn't show them to you. I'm not taking any responsibility. Okay?"

"Okay. Let's do it."

So he walked into his office, where I saw him shuffling some papers for a couple minutes. Then he left, leaving the records lying open on his desk. It wasn't hard to find my three players' names; each of them had cashed checks in that place—checks that came from agents, checks that verified my players had been bought. I had my confirmation.

I came forward with what I had and two of my players got suspended. The NCAA investigated, but didn't look at players from any other schools. The investigation continued after the season was over, however, and turned up about thirty guys from other teams who had received checks—but my players were the only ones ever suspended.

Chris Mortensen told me the agents were worried about me, that they didn't like me turning up the heat. I received threatening phone calls at home; anonymous callers promised they would destroy my reputation, try to spread damaging rumors. Chris told me they would come after me, and that it wasn't just the agents who were concerned; it was also the men the agents were working for, the people backing them: the mob.

One of the agents was Lloyd Bloom. Bloom was not a bad agent; he was just a stupid agent. He was the flip guy, the face-to-face liaison with players. He would ply players with money and gifts and other bribes. Bloom "flipped" the players, convincing them to sign. He bought their trust, got into their lives, and sold them out.

Chris Mortensen, the FBI, and others finally exposed enough of the operations to get Bloom arrested and tried. Bloom eventually admitted that the mob was behind some of the recruiting, trying to infiltrate college football to fix games. Bloom went public and ended up murdered. As I said, he wasn't a bad guy, just stupid. Because of the campaign waged by me, other coaches, and other leaders, the NCAA designed better rules and restrictions to control the agents by making them register and have some official accountability. But the controversy goes on even today. I suppose it will always be a problem until college football programs, the NCAA, and the NFL find a way to work together.

On April 19, 1988, the *New York Times*, in its "Sports People" feature, reported:

UNUSUAL BONUS

Mike Gottfried, the University of Pittsburgh football coach, signed a long-term guaranteed contract yesterday that the school's athletic director, Edward

Bozik, called unique in college football because it would pay a bonus based on the graduation rate of players. Neither Bozik nor Gottfried would disclose the agreement's length or financial terms. Bozik said it contained a bonus for bowl seasons.

After my third winning season at Pitt, the administration offered me a lifetime contract. The AD and Chancellor Wesley Posvar sat down with me and said, "We want you to be the head coach of the University of Pittsburgh for the rest of your life. Are you interested? Joe Paterno's up at Penn State, and he's shown that consistency is important. We've lost Johnny Majors, Jackie Sherrill. We've fired folks. We want a coach for life. What do you think?"

Many big schools had experienced some success with long-term coaches, but lifetime, rollover contracts were still a fairly new deal in the NCAA. The consistency and loyalty that develops under a coach with a long tenure tends to help a program, since the player rosters always change. Having someone stay at the helm for an extended period can make a program solid.

The offer really made me think. Like Paterno or Bo Schembechler at Michigan, I could plant myself at Pitt and serve out the rest of my career there. I had constantly been moving my family around the country since I started coaching—a year here, a few years there. It was rough on my family. But now, we could plant some roots, let the kids settle in, and make Pittsburgh our permanent home.

And I knew I could win at Pitt. I'd done it already. I'd

turned the team around and put it on the right track, and I knew we could keep it going. I could build on the good recruiting we'd done. Despite some of the problems and politics, it was a good job. NCAA coaching was changing, so I knew I couldn't avoid the difficult stuff, anyway. If I wanted to coach a big school, it came with the territory. So I decided to take the offer.

The assistant AD, Dean Billick, later told me they had worked for more than a year to come up with that contract so that I would stay around; they didn't want to lose me. It was a great contract, with great incentives and stability for the future. I signed it, they signed it, and it was done.

My problems, however, were not. The moment would come when I would pray to get out of that lifetime contract.

■

Soon afterward, some academics got the chancellor's ear, trying to convince him to raise the standards for admission to the university in an attempt to become part of the academic elite. They wanted to raise the academic bar above Ohio State, above West Virginia, above a lot of the other schools against whom we competed.

These folks wanted the minimum ACT scores to go up two points, and they wanted a minimum score of 850 on the SAT. That may not seem like a big deal, and it may, in fact, benefit an institution such as the University of Pittsburgh—but for a football program or for athletes in general, it's not good news. Pitt had a history of being a heavy player in football, and its constituents demanded a winning program, led by a winning head coach. But now the academics threatened to shake all that up by changing the entrance standards. And it wouldn't affect the football program alone; every sport would take a big hit. It would have put us at a definite disadvantage with Penn State, Ohio State, West Virginia, Notre Dame—all the schools that operated under the same NCAA rules that governed us.

Several Pitt coaches got together and approached me, wanting to fight the idea. They agreed that the new standards would hurt all of the athletic programs, but since Pitt was about football more than anything else, they came to me, hoping I'd lead the charge. Paul Evans, the basketball coach, said it all: "Gottfried, you have a lifetime contract. None of us do. We need you to head this thing up." On the other hand, Dean Billick advised me to drop the whole thing and not risk getting on the wrong side of the administration.

When I decided it was important enough to fight, I jumped into another mess, putting myself at odds with the administration and making myself a target for more criticism and complaints. Every coach has to put up with criticism, but when I took up the conflict with the academics, I knew I was asking for it. It quickly got ugly and it made my job a trial, not a joy. I began to wonder what God was up to. I began to wonder if I should stick around.

It happened after the Navy game at Pitt in 1989. We had won, so there was a lot of celebrating, as usual. The crowd was cheering, the players were happy and excited. But as I walked off the field, something just didn't feel right. Here I was, at one of the best football schools in the nation, doing what I had always dreamed of doing. And I was winning! But the struggles and politics and controversy were all taking a toll. I prayed something that I never thought I would: "Lord, I need you to get me out of here." I actually prayed to leave Pitt.

I knew then that it was time for me to go.

Pastor Joseph Garlington has taught me that we need to make our prayers specific. I learned that lesson the hard way. I should have prayed something like "Lord, I need you to get me out of here—but I'd like to go peacefully, please. And I'd like to continue to be a coach somewhere." But that's not what I prayed. God took my prayer as seriously as I had prayed it, and He answered that prayer.

Confrontation with the administration over various aspects of the program did not let up my whole time at Pitt. Somehow along the way, I fell out of favor with Chancellor Posvar. More and more, I seemed to be a burr in his saddle, and the chafing continued to worsen. At the second and final Emerald Isle Classic in Dublin, Ireland, the conflict reached the point where I just said to myself, *That's enough.*

In place of a game against Rutgers at their place, we played them in Ireland as a public relations event promoting NCAA football. On December 2, 1989, at Lansdowne Road Stadium, we took on Rutgers in front of more than forty thousand fans.

Before the game the referees had told me, "We're on TV back in Pittsburgh and all over, so timing is tight." The stadium in Dublin didn't have locker rooms, and Rutgers got the locker room closest to the stadium. Pitt got a locker room a fifteen-minute walk away. The referee warned me, "Mike, get them out there on time. Start walking early, because we will start this game on time; and if you're not there, we'll penalize you."

At halftime, we took the fifteen-minute walk back to the locker room, where game business gets done with the team. It's a private place where coaches and players can make crucial adjustments. But when we got there, I noticed a loud contingent in the corner making a racket. The chancellor and a PR group he brought over for the game had gathered in the locker room for the thrill of being there, and they were behaving in what I took to be an inappropriate way (and not for the first time).

Locker rooms, however, are not good places for parties with your friends. Not my locker rooms, anyway.

I had to work out a game plan for the second half, gather information from my coaches, and talk to my players—and I needed to do it all and get back to the stadium in time. The presence of the corner PR group did not sit well with me, so I sent the manager, Speck, to deliver a curt message: "Tell those people to hold the noise down!" I didn't know if my little manager could manage it, but he went straight over to the chancellor, looked him in the eye and said, "Would you guys hold the noise down, please?" That move didn't make me any friends among the corner power bunch.

Speck came back to me with a message: "Chancellor Posvar

wants Sophie Masloff to speak to the team before we go back to the stadium." Sophie Masloff was the mayor of Pittsburgh at the time, but I couldn't believe the request. It simply wasn't what was supposed to go on in the locker room during half-time. The chancellor and the mayor wanted to use my halftime in the locker room as a PR media moment—and I couldn't allow it.

"No," I told Speck, "that ain't gonna happen." I didn't send Speck back with the message; I just ignored the request and went on with my plans. The officials insisted we had to be right on time, and so I called up all the players and told them what to do. Then I said, "Send them out." I simply didn't have time for a mayoral speech.

My actions angered Chancellor Posvar, but I was concerned only about one thing: winning the game. That was my job. That's what the university paid me to do. That's why I was in Ireland. I didn't worry about the chancellor or the politics of the situation.

I should have worried.

By the time of that game, the last of the season, I had already landed on my boss's bad side. I should probably have handled the situation better, and I regret what I did. Still, in its first-ever game overseas, Pitt defeated Rutgers, 46–29.

It was the last football game of my coaching career.

I had no idea they were going to fire me.

I should have seen it coming. I knew that the chancellor

wanted me out. I had put up too much of a stink about the proposed academic requirements, and he didn't like me pushing against him. But everybody else at the school was in my corner, and that's why it surprised me. There were warning signs, however, that should have clued me in.

I had been recruiting all that week and came home on December 12 to get ready to play in the John Hancock Bowl against Texas A&M. Ed Bozik, the AD, came into my office looking a little pale. "Mike, Kentucky just called for permission to talk to you," he said. "You are not going to talk to them, are you?"

I said yes. Then he turned and slammed the door in anger. He didn't want me to speak to Kentucky.

On December 14, I got a call from Ray Anthony. "Mike, everything all right?" he asked. Ray was an avid Pitt fan and a good friend. He owned the largest crane company in America. He had a circle of wealthy friends who had the ear of the chancellor, so he had some inside knowledge—but he decided not to tell me what was up, a decision he later regretted.

"Sure," I answered, "everything's good, Ray."

"No," he pushed back, "I mean, *is everything all right?*"

I didn't understand his meaning, and I wouldn't understand until later. "It's good, Ray. Everything's good."

Eventually I learned that the AD and his people had been talking to the chancellor for days, trying desperately to get him to change his mind. Dr. Posvar had decided to fire me, and Ray must have heard the news. He knew my circumstances were about to change. If I had known, I could have called some friends, put the pressure on, maybe saved my job. But I didn't know until the very end.

On December 15, 1989, after a winning season and just days before a bowl game, the University of Pittsburgh declared me legally dead.

I walked into the AD's office and Ed said, "How are you feeling?" He asked it as if he expected me to be ill.

"I'm feeling good. Everything's going well." Even as I spoke, I sensed that something was bothering Ed, so I said, "Well, Ed, tell me how *you* are feeling."

"I'm not feeling real well."

I knew he had a bad heart and so I worried about him. "What's wrong?"

"Just not feeling good." Then, out of the clear blue sky, with no more pleasantries or any more warning than that, he said, "Mike, we want you to resign, or we're going to fire you."

I felt in total shock. You could have knocked me down with a feather. The way Ed had been acting, I thought that maybe *he* was going to resign. In fact, it had occurred to me that, because of his poor health, maybe he was about to pass the AD torch to me. And instead, I was being fired.

I remained speechless for a minute, until finally I said to him, "What are the reasons?"

"Well, we're . . . we'll . . . Look. There are no reasons." He gave me nothing. "Mike, we're just changing directions. We're just going in a different direction."

I knew exactly what *that* meant. When someone tells you,

"We're going in a different direction," what they really mean is that you're not going with them. I wanted to say to Ed, "Hey! Just tell me what direction you intend to go, and I'll go right along with you." But that wasn't what he was saying at all. He'd just given me the ax.

Pitt had given me the contract of a lifetime through a lifetime contract. Now, they had declared me legally dead.

"Mike," he continued, "we'll let you coach the last game, the bowl game, if you'll just agree to not fight your contract."

Now they were threatening to take away the bowl game from me! I wanted to coach that game, but not under a deal like that. I stood up and walked to the door. "Ed," I said, "I'm not going for that." And then I walked out of the room. That's the last time I ever talked to Ed Bozik.

I went home and told Mickey what had happened. A close friend came over to the house, and while he was there, a big winter storm blew in. We talked all night.

Later I learned that nobody in the administration wanted me fired, except one person. Ed Bozik didn't want it. His assistant didn't want it. The vice chancellor didn't want it. The only one who wanted me gone was Chancellor Posvar, and he got his way.

For three days after my firing, Pittsburgh remained snowed under. The night of December 15, the press camped outside my house to get my reaction, but I didn't come out. Dean Billick told me later that the group of university administrators all watched TV together that night to see how I would play things. But since I didn't talk to the press, and the university didn't say much more, that made the media itchy to get to the heart of the story.

When the media started to pressure the university brass, the school suddenly had to come up with reasons for letting me go. The chancellor told the assistant AD, "Okay, Dean, draw up four reasons why we fired him."

"But I didn't fire him," Dean said.

"Just pick out four things, Dean, any four things."

He told me later, "Mike, I just threw those four things together out of the blue." The press reported these four things as the reason I left Pitt: the academic issue; the budget; poor public relations; and poor media relations.

Under advice from legal counsel, I didn't make a stink about being fired. In fact, I didn't say anything at all. That's the biggest mistake I made. My contract stipulated that if I made a big deal out of things, the contract could be revoked. The university desperately wanted the contract revoked, and it was just waiting for me to cause some trouble. The contract stipulated that I be paid for four years after severance, and the administration didn't want to have to spend that money. But I fought for it.

The lack of solid information and real reasons for my dismissal from the university made the newspaper writers angry. They wanted to know why a guy with a good record was getting canned. They thought there must be something more besides what they were being fed. So the media launched an investigation to figure out why I got dismissed.

The media frenzy prompted a separate investigation by the

NCAA. The university wouldn't say anything, I wasn't talking for fear of voiding the contract, and the press and the NCAA were poking around everywhere, looking into anything that might explain what happened. The investigation went on for four years. Every facet of the football program—rules, violations, academics—everything got picked through. Of course, if the university had anything to use against me in a legitimate way—if I'd broken any rules at all—it could have squeezed out of the contract and stopped paying me. Instead, it had nothing; but for four long years, I lived under a cloud of suspicion.

Dave Didion, an investigator with the NCAA, told me the whole investigation never should have happened. Dave Swank, the chairman of the NCAA Committee on Infractions, eventually apologized to me, but his mea culpa got no media coverage. The NCAA put the Pitt basketball team on probation after finding some violations there, but it didn't find anything—not even a single infraction—in the entire football program that presented any kind of problem.

On December 30, 1989, in the locker room before the John Hancock Bowl, Paul Hackett, my offensive coordinator, was named head coach. Pitt won the game against Texas A&M, 31–28. Nine Panther starters never made it to the next season; either they were dismissed by the new coach, they turned pro, they flunked out, or they transferred.

More than twenty coaches called to express their sympathy for my firing. John Ralston, the legendary coach at Stanford (and later the Broncos), gave me sage advice: "Mike, the one thing you'll have to get used to is not being part of a team any-more."

"What do you mean?" I wondered.

"Well, you've been a part of a team in grade school, and high school, and college, and as a coach. And now, all of a sudden, you're not on a team."

John was exactly right. In the following years, I discovered I had an intrinsic need to be part of a team.

Getting fired wasn't the worst day of my life, but it was close. I had worked hard to get there, all the way to coaching a big team such as Pitt. That was my dream. That's all I ever wanted to do. I had made it, it was working, and I was making a difference—and all of a sudden, *bam!* Just like that, it was all over.

I started asking the same questions that had hammered me when my dad had died and again when Marcy had almost died at birth. I prayed the same prayers, all centered on "Why?"

I guess I wish I could have left another way, but I had prayed for it to happen. Despite everything, however, I still felt I wasn't done with coaching. I had no doubt that I'd come back and coach somewhere. It wasn't over!

But the Lord had other plans.

Once again, I faced a choice: would I trust God in the losses of my life, as well as the wins? It was easy to trust God's plan as a winning coach. But when I suffered a profound loss, I found myself back in the roundhouse, with crucial decisions to make.

I had to face another death, this time the death of my dreams. And the promise God had given me, first spoken by a Catholic nun back in the sixth grade at St. Joseph's, ran through my heart once again:

"'For I know the plans I have for you,' says the LORD, 'plans to prosper you and not to harm you, plans to give you a hope and a future.'"

FILL THE GAP

One day I was walking the halls of Congress, talking to important and influential people, when I received a call from one of my boys. I didn't put him on hold or make him leave a message. I took the call. Why? Because I've told these boys I would be there for them—and I mean what I say.

I refuse to tell these boys I'm going to be there for them, then not answer when they call. Not many people are more important to me than my boys!

Maybe I'm having lunch with Pete Rose when the phone rings. I'll grab my cell, and there will be a boy on the other end, having some kind of problem or just wanting to talk. Sometimes he wants to tell me he got an A on his report card or did well at his after-school job. Or he wants my advice on college plans, or he wants to tell me he made twenty free throws in a row. So I take the call—and then after talking to him for a minute, I hand the phone to Pete Rose and have *him* talk to my boy. Who doesn't get a kick out of *that*?

Another day I was in Texas, out to dinner with Coach Mack Brown of the University of Texas. We met right before the Longhorns won a national championship by defeating top-ranked USC in the 2005 Rose Bowl. During the meal Davis called me. I excused myself from the dinner conversation and spoke to Davis for a few minutes. Then I said, "Hold on, Davis. I want you to talk to Mack Brown."

Davis knew *exactly* who Mack Brown was. I told Mack,

"This is one of our Team Focus boys. He's a good football player." And then I passed the phone to Mack, who spoke with Davis for about five minutes. They talked about football and about the big game coming up. Davis couldn't believe it. Here he was, talking on a cell phone to the coach of one of the best college football teams in the country!

Yesterday my cell phone rang seven times, and each time a boy was on the other end. All they wanted was someone to talk to. All they needed was someone who would listen. Each of them was looking to fill a space, and I did my best to stand in for their missing dads.

For those boys to know that someone will pick up the phone at the other end, someone who knows their name, who knows what's going on in their life, and who knows what the struggle looks and feels like—well, that makes an enormous difference.

Ask any football coach, "Coach, how do you win a game?" and he'll be sure to answer, "One play at a time." That's how we're going to reach this generation: one boy at a time.

I don't go in for numbers. God will take care of how many boys we have in Team Focus and how we'll fly them in for camps and how we'll pay for it all. I just know He wants me to reach out to the next boy, the one who doesn't have a functional father, and tell him, "You're great. I love you. You belong here on this team, in this family."

This burning desire grows in me as each new boy gets added to the team. It burns in me whenever I feel the emptiness in my own heart.

Does it burn in you, too?

ESPN once asked me to cover a spring game at Harvard. They didn't think I'd want to go, but I jumped at the chance. Hey, why not? It's the only way I'd ever get to Harvard!

I felt quite impressed, not only with the campus, but also with the football program. I was standing on the field when a young black man came by. Soon I started talking to him.

"Are you a player?"

"Yes, sir, I'm a running back."

I don't know what it was, but my radar picked up something about him. I can usually detect a missing-father gap. So I asked point-blank, "Hey, do you have a father?"

"No, sir. My father died when I was two years old." He then told me about being born in Canada and about some of his growing-up years.

"Hey, I got something for you to think about," I said. "I want you to come to Washington, D.C., and talk to a group of boys. It's a camp called Team Focus, just for boys without dads. You're a Harvard football player, going to be a pro someday. You'd be great."

He didn't blink. "I'll do it. I'll be there."

And so Clifton Dawson came to the D.C. camp to work from 7 a.m. to 1 a.m. for five whole days, helping out in all kinds of ways. At the end of camp, I gave him a check for $150—not much as an honorarium. He gave me a hug and said, "I've had a great time, Coach." Then he went to work at another camp.

Ten days later when I returned home, I found a card waiting for me with a check inside. Clifton had sent back the $150! Now, this was a twenty-year- old college student. I knew he could use the money. But he returned it with an explanation: "Coach, I got more out of the camp than I could ever get in money. I appreciate being asked to come. Thank you."

That's the way it is when you give your life to a boy who needs you. You can't buy the feeling of knowing you've helped a young man turn a crucial corner in his life. Instead of living down to the statistics, because of you he can find and live out his God-given destiny.

And by the way, your own life will never be the same, either.

CHAPTER NINE

LANDING AT ESPN

was out of a job, but at least I knew my phone worked. It just kept ringing and ringing.

Once again, I was forced to lean back and trust God and His plans for my future. By now I'd been through enough in my life that I should have been able to trust Him without asking questions like "Why?" and "What are you doing with me?" But I asked them anyway.

His answer was quick in coming.

The news that I had been fired got around fast. In fact, the information was leaked to certain media four days before the school told me. Maybe that explains why on the day after I lost my job, I got five phone calls from ESPN, all of them asking me to audition as an on-air college football analyst.

Mickey and I talked it over. It seemed worth a shot. I thought I could do it, even though I'd never done anything like it. I had a good knowledge of college ball and the various teams and personalities that any analyst needs, and I loved the game. I also brought something extra: a coaching perspective. In fact, the job ESPN was offering fit me perfectly. I figured, *Why not try something different in between coaching jobs?* So I agreed to the audition.

Tim Brando, an announcer on ESPN's studio show, met me in Bristol, Connecticut, the home of the network. Tim was a friend from way back and seemed excited that I might come to work there. He talked me through several issues and helped me with the audition. His counsel must have taken, because I did well enough that they offered me the job. I took it.

I was to meet the rest of the crew in Bristol the following August for the fall meetings, the preparatory event for the football season at ESPN. As the time drew closer, however, I started getting nervous about the whole thing, because I didn't have much time to get ready. I knew I could handle the football aspect of the job, but I had always been a coach; take me out of that setting, and I felt lost.

I started to feel sorry for myself. *What am I doing?* I asked myself. *I shouldn't be doing this.* On my way out the door for the meeting I said to Mickey, "I'm not feeling good about this." I called her when I arrived in Bristol and said once more, "I really don't know if I belong here."

"Well, is there anybody you know there?" Mickey asked most sensibly. "You could talk to someone and see how they feel about it."

"Yeah, Lee Corso's here. He's a good friend. That's a great

idea, Mick! I'm gonna call him." I hung up and immediately called Lee Corso's room. Lee is a lead football announcer at ESPN and I'd known him for years. When I explained that I just wanted to talk things over with him, Lee said he'd tell me everything I needed to know.

Lee walked early every morning, so I got up at 6:30 a.m. and took a walk with him. He had on his tennis shoes, ready to do some power walking. "Okay," he said, "I'm gonna tell you everything you need to know about working for ESPN." He walked a little faster and I scrambled to keep up.

"Number one," he said, "after you do a game, you're going to come down from the booth and you're going to say to the crew, 'How'd I do?' And no matter who you ask, they'll say, 'You did a great job!' They'll hit you on the back and say, 'Great job, Buddy!' But they don't mean it."

He walked a little faster and I continued to chase him. "They don't mean it, Mike. Just know that. They don't mean it at all. And here's the second thing: as soon as somebody gets hired with a bigger name than you, and that's gonna be *any-body*"—Lee laughed while he walked— "as soon as that happens, you're gonna be outta here. They're gonna hire him and move you out."

I stretched my stride to keep up with his brisk pace. "Okay," I said, "anything else?" Lee had years of experience, so I knew he could give me hours of his wisdom. "What else do I need to know?"

"That's it. That's all you need to know about working at ESPN."

The network signed me for five games that first season, offering me a conditional first-year contract, meaning that for the first year I was on probation. It was just a trial to see how I'd work out. Plus, they knew I wanted to return to coaching.

I was a coach from the bottom of my shoes to the top of my head, and most important, in my heart. Coaching was my life, and for me there was no higher calling, no other mountain to climb, no occupation or hobby more endearing. Football coaching was *it* for me.

I loved coaching not just for the love of the game, but also for the team atmosphere, for the thrill of putting a plan together and getting a win. Most of all, I loved coaching because of the guys. I enjoyed working with college players, developing them and watching them come along, not only in athletics, but in their maturity as men. Working with the players—that was the most exciting thing of all.

I took the job at ESPN knowing that as soon as an appealing coaching job opened up, I'd take it and be gone. I had no intention of staying long, and that sense stuck with me. I even prayed for a coaching job. I prayed that God would give me the desires of my heart, and my desire was to coach. In the meantime, while I waited for God to come through, I joined ESPN as an analyst. I determined to give it my best shot.

I had reason to feel nervous about my new assignment. I'd never done TV and I tend to mangle the King's English. The folks at ESPN never worked with me to tell me what to expect, nor did they ever help me with reading, speaking, and listening to the voice in my earpiece. Nobody ever told me, "Hey, we're going to be talking to you right in your ear while you're describing the game to millions of sports fans." Nobody practiced with me. They just threw me in on the first game, cold turkey.

My first game took place in Hawaii. I was a bundle of nerves. It was time to sink or swim—but first, I had to find the stadium.

I got lost on my way to the first game of my sports television career. As a college football coach, I never had to think about the whereabouts of a stadium; I always rode a bus! Somebody who knew the way drove me to every game. But now, my first game for ESPN, I got lost. I thought, *This is just great.*

Finally I and the other ESPN staffer with me saw the stadium *over there*, but we kept missing the exit. The network wanted us there two hours ahead of the game. We eventually arrived, but late.

When I got to the control booth, they handed me my earpiece. The guys who produce the show from the truck speak in your ear during the game, giving prompts and cues, telling you what to do, what to mention, that kind of thing. Everything comes into the announcers through the earpiece. And I had no idea about any of it.

Hawaii kicked off, Texas A&M returned the ball to the 20-yard line, and the play-by-play guy, Sean McDonough, started talking. I was ready to go, anxious to say something, wondering what I would say. But Sean kept talking, so I let him go, waiting for my chance.

When Texas came out of the huddle, I got myself ready. On the team's first play, the A&M guy ran for four yards. I was standing on the edge of my toes, ready to say something, *anything*, and all of a sudden Sean McDonough said, "Ladies and gentlemen, let me give you the starting offensive lineup for Texas A&M." I remained silent while he read all the names.

As Sean neared the end of list, I geared up to speak. A&M broke from the huddle and ran for three yards. Just as I got ready to open my mouth, Sean said, "Ladies and gentlemen, let me give you the defensive starting lineup for Hawaii." So he went through all those names. At that point I began to wonder if I'd ever be able to jump in and do my job.

On the third play, Robert Wilson, a stocky little Texas running back who looked like a Coke machine, picked up fifteen yards. In my ear the producer said, "Okay, Coach, tell the American people why that play worked."

"All right," I replied.

In my earpiece I heard all kinds of shock and shuffling and commotion from the truck, and the producer barked in my ear, "You can't say 'all right'! You just said 'all right' to sixty million people!"

So I said, "Okay."

Of course, 60 million people heard that comment, too, and that's the way it went for a little while. I kept talking, having a conversation with the producer as he spoke into my ear, telling me to end our little dialogue and instead talk to America.

I never got to say anything about that play. By the time I was ready, the moment had passed and we were on to the next down.

When I finally jumped in and said something, I butchered it. I just fractured the English language. Still I kept it up, talking in half sentences and unfinished phrases, getting names wrong. I guess I did all right—at least that's what Mickey tells me—but it felt as if I were messing up the whole show. I'm not an especially talkative guy and I wasn't used to speaking for three and a half hours at a stretch. I simply didn't know what I was doing.

After the game I came down from the booth, demoralized. I asked the crew, "So—how'd I do?"

"Great!" they all said. "Did a great job, buddy! Welcome to the team!" And they patted me on the back. Immediately Lee Corso's words came back to me. *Great,* I thought, *that's just great.*

It's a miracle I lasted more than a week.

After my first five games, the network brass thought I'd improved tremendously and done a great job for them, and ESPN wanted to move me right into the Saturday-night prime-time slot. So they offered me a longer contract. "We want to give you a lifetime contract!" they kidded me.

"Hey," I replied, "I've fallen for that one once, and I know what that means."

Someone once told me, "A lifetime contract works like this: when you lose, they're gonna kill you." ESPN offered me a five-year contract, and I took it. I was the first ESPN announcer with a buyout clause in my contract, which stipulated that if I ever went back to coaching, I'd pay them back. That meant it would cost me some money.

But I still prayed to go back.

Since joining ESPN, I've been approached about coaching jobs at Cincinnati, Kentucky, South Carolina, LSU, and other schools. Temple University offered me its head-coaching position. I decided the job was worth seriously looking into, so I took the next step and visited the campus and met with the AD. Before I left home, I said to Mickey, "If I see even one thing at Temple that I like, I will take the job."

I didn't see one thing I liked, and so I stayed with ESPN. God planned it that way.

Working for ESPN has given me perspective. When I began, ESPN was a newcomer and didn't yet have the respect of the industry, as CBS or ABC did. In those days, when we came to a game, they'd shuffle us to the end of the table. Even then, though, I knew ESPN was going to make it and that I could have a good future there. Still, I entertained the thought *Maybe I should quit before it's too late and go back to coaching.*

But I'd talk to the coaches. Because I'd been a coach for so many years, coaches would open up to me and let me know what was going on. Many coaches shared with me the great pressure they were constantly under to win, to produce. They always felt the full weight of any problems that developed. The job of a college football coach was changing. More was expected of them—more media exposure, more fund-raising, more schmoozing with benefactors. And now I was in a position to give these coaches some advice and perspective.

"Don't worry about the problems," I told these friends. "Enjoy the good days and smile. Enjoy the game." I tried to encourage them and tell them how their team was getting better. I tried to be as positive as I could.

After a game, I'd see the winning coach pumping his fist in the air and I'd think, *Boy, I miss those feelings.* But then, out of the corner of my eye, I'd see the other coach—the losing one—slumped over, shuffling out the other end of the field, and I'd think, *I sure don't miss that. That guy's going to a press conference where they're gonna ask him all kinds of tough questions. He's in for a rough night.*

I had tasted what it felt like to coach with the elite schools, and I liked it. I would have returned to coaching at nearly any college, not just a big one, because I loved it. But God has not moved me back in that direction. For all kinds of reasons, I have yet to accept a coaching position offered to me.

For a long time I prayed, "Lord, You say in Your book that You will give us the desires of our hearts. The one desire of my heart is to go back and coach." Even today, the desire sometimes springs up without warning. But when it does, one thing keeps me from pursuing it. God has given me a new passion, a different burning desire in my heart. But it's taken time for me to see it.

After I took the job at ESPN, we moved to Mobile, Alabama. I said to Mickey, "We'll be here for one year, and then I'll get a coaching job." That was my assumption, that we wouldn't be staying long. Despite my five-year contract with ESPN, I didn't think I'd last the whole time. I was ready to coach and I kept praying that it would happen soon.

Those first years in Mobile, I didn't get involved in many local activities because I firmly believed I was going to move on soon. I was in transit and didn't want to put down roots. I had no desire to get involved in the community. I had done a lot of that during my coaching years—speaking at Rotary Clubs, going to banquets, being part of the local sports scene. But I was done with all that. In Mobile I just wanted a break, so I avoided the spotlight.

But my work with ESPN gave me a lot of free time. It wasn't like coaching. Coaching kept me busy all the time; something always needed to be done, all year long. Now, it felt as though I had all the time in the world, especially in the off-season.

Mickey could see my restlessness, so she pulled me aside one day to offer her advice: "I'm going to tell you what you need to do. You need to read your Bible, you need to study up, you need to pray. You have a lot of time on your hands right now, time that you're not used to, and you need to make the most of it."

Mickey saw a need in my life—a need to get closer to God, to take my relationship to Jesus Christ more seriously.

From my days growing up in St. Joseph's Church, I've

always loved Jesus Christ and considered Him my Savior. I've considered myself a Christian, a follower of Jesus. I haven't always done what I should, but when I've blown it, I've asked God for forgiveness. But God had still more work that He wanted to do in me, and now He had arranged for some time in my life that would allow me to make some needed changes.

I followed my wife's advice—something I suggest all husbands do—and started spending time reading and studying the Bible and praying. Over long walks I talked to God, in real conversations. Something began to happen, not all of a sudden, but gradually, as I used the time to better get to know God. He was changing me.

Rey Dempsey had been a good coaching friend for years. He had experienced a radical conversion, a "Damascus Road" kind of thing, and he was born-again, eventually becoming a pastor. To Mickey and me, Rey took the role of a spiritual mentor, so when got together, the conversation invariably turned to Christ.

Up to that time, I was politely interested in what had happened to Rey, but I wasn't ready to make any radical commitments myself. At one point, parked along a road in southern Illinois, Rey told me about what God had done in his life. I reached over, patted Rey's hand, and said, "That's great for you, Rey." I considered Rey's experience valid and good, but I didn't see how it had much to do with me. Hey, I was already a Christian.

Sometime later, Mickey and I were sitting in a swing on the porch of Rey's home in Columbus, Ohio, enjoying an evening with Rey and his wife. Once more Rey talked about his conversion and what it meant to be a follower of Jesus Christ. After several minutes, Rey's wife said, "Rey, can I say something?" He nodded and she looked at me. "Mike, do you want to make Jesus your Savior and Lord, or do you not? That's what it comes down to."

The porch swing stopped midswing as I contemplated the point-blank question. It wasn't as if I'd ever turned my back on God. It wasn't that I'd stopped believing or stopped wanting to obey. I knew I was a Christian, that I believed in Jesus. But I knew that my faith in Christ—the ongoing, vital, day-to-day relationship—needed a change. Jesus needed to be Lord in several areas of my life where He hadn't been before. I had not allowed the depth of His forgiveness to penetrate into the deepest places of my heart. Did I want what Rey and his wife had? Did I want to make Jesus Christ the Lord and Master of *all* of me? I answered the question.

"Yes. Yes, I do."

In Mobile, I finally had the time to pursue that relationship. God's plans—the plans He had for me from the very beginning, the plans I had entrusted to Him over the years, the plans "not to harm, but to prosper," plans "for a hope and a future"— were about to unfold into something I had never imagined and would not have pursued, except that I now was spending time to get to know my Lord.

He was changing the desires of my heart . . . and those desires would be tested.

Whenever Mickey and I are going somewhere, whether out to dinner or on a trip, I always look for someone to join us—a habit I learned from my dad. Several years ago, after I began a ministry for boys without fathers, Mickey and I took two high-school guys, Davis and Rueben, on a skiing vacation to Vail, Colorado. (Mickey claims I just wanted a few friends along for a snowball fight. She's probably right.) While there, I got a call from Cincinnati.

Dean Billick, the former assistant athletic director at Pitt, now working the same job at Cincinnati, explained that they were looking for a new head coach. "Mike," he said, "we believe you can get this job if you want it."

I got off the phone, excited. Ohio is my home, and they were offering me a comeback job. I could be a head coach again, for a team with a great history and a great program. Ideas and plans and players and plays raced through my head. Mickey could tell right away that something big was up.

"What are you so excited about?" she asked.

"Guess what? That was Cincinnati, and they want me to coach. I could go to work as their head coach!"

Mickey looked at me for a moment, unwilling to burst my bubble. But she knew I hadn't thought through everything all the way. Then she asked me a simple question that I still ask whenever a school looking for a coach contacts me.

"What about the boys?" She came over and put her hand on my shoulder. "Do you remember what you said to those boys?"

"What's that?" I wondered, thinking she might be talking about Rueben or Davis.

"You said you're going to walk with them, be there for them. Can you take this job and still be true to your promise to the boys?"

I thought about it, but only for a moment. I thought about Rueben and Davis. I thought about all the other boys I'd come to know and love. I thought about all the boys all over the country who had lost their dad and needed some help, someone to help fill the father space.

"You're right, Mick," I said at last. "I can't do this."

I returned Dean's call and told him I wouldn't be interested in the job. "You know I'd love to coach in Cincinnati, and I'd love to live there," I said. "Ohio is my home. But I can't leave what I'm doing now; I know I can't leave it. I know where I'm supposed to be, and I know I'm doing things that are more important than winning football games."

Sounds confident, doesn't it? But even though I meant what I said, I still felt as if I might have made a mistake, that maybe I should call Dean again and tell him I was interested in the job after all. I thought about it all that night, wrestling with my decision. It finally occurred to me that night that I *had* settled the thing. Between God and me, the decision had been made, and it was the right one. I knew this was true: *coaching football was not my future and not God's plan.* I knew it that night. God had made it plain.

I haven't stopped coaching, however. Now I just do it for a different team, in a much more important game. As I look over my life, I believe I was supposed to work with these boys. All of this—my growing-up years, the loss of my father, my experience coaching, working at Pitt, being fired, getting the job at ESPN—all of it prepared me for this time in my life. God has worked His plan from the very beginning, and it has given me the chance to work with these boys, to coach their lives and not just their sport.

I have been given a calling to step into the picture of a boy's life and into the gap where his father should be, and try to help. My whole life pointed in this direction, and here I am. God has given me the desire of my heart—and I never saw it coming.

Oh, I still get the coaching bug. A couple of times I've seen Rey Dempsey—who also got fired from his football coaching position—and I've asked him, "Do you miss coaching, Rey?" He always gives the same answer: "I have to be obedient." That's the bottom line.

And that night in Colorado, I went outside, grabbed some snow, packed it into a nice, big ball, and went off to find a couple of boys for a fight.

FILL THE GAP

When I was young, I'd often see boys talking to their dads after a practice or a game and I'd think, *Boy, that would be great. Just to go over and share with him, talk to him about the game, about my life. To sit with my dad and have a Coke or a milk shake and say, "Dad, what do you think? What could I do better?"*

But instead I'd go home by myself and sit there and think, *Who am I going to talk this over with? Mom's working, my brothers are gone, and I'm all alone.*

Growing into adulthood didn't take away my loneliness. As a head coach, I've gone to meetings in restaurants dressed in a shirt and a sport coat, and somebody would say to me, "Hey, you have to wear a tie to go in there." It's not that I don't own a tie, but I still can't tie one, so I have to find somebody to tie the thing for me—a janitor or a busboy or a friend. And every time it happens, a little piece of the pain comes back to remind me of what I missed.

Too many times to count, I'd be sitting somewhere in a locker room, getting ready to play another game or preparing to lead my players as head coach, and I would ache for my father. Standing on the sidelines at Notre Dame or Penn State while the national anthem was being played, I'd feel the emotion welling up, and a tear would run down my cheek. And so I'd say to anyone who happened to be near, "Boy, I wish my dad was here to see this."

Mom would always say, "He's watching you from above." And I know that's true; I've never doubted it for a minute. I'm certain my father is in heaven and I'm glad he's there. But just knowing that truth doesn't take away the emptiness of not having a flesh-and-blood person right here, right now—at your side in a real-life relationship—helping, encouraging, supporting. You can go through all kinds of things in your life, whether good or bad, and even though you know he's up there, if somebody's not here to go through it with you, it's just not as good.

Sure, you can get over the hump of it. You can get to the place where your loss doesn't define everything about you. The love of Jesus can heal the pain you feel. If you have good support from others, you can fill the gap in your life with excellent things. But the emotional absence, the void of Dad not being around? It's always there.

I still think about it whenever I visit Crestline. I think of it when I watch my kids and my grandkids: *My dad never got to see any of us all grown-up. He never got the sense of joy and fulfillment that comes from playing with his grandchildren.* Every once in a while, that little, aching emptiness bubbles to the surface.

I know the emptiness will never disappear, but there is always hope. I never lost hope. I got angry and I felt hurt. I worried about the future. But I never completely lost hope.

Why not? That's not hard to answer.

I attribute my ability to hang on to hope to the influencers in my life, to the significant people around me: the men of Crestline, Coach Hutson, my college coaches, and so many others. All built me up instead of tearing me down. Collectively, they supplied the five things that can fill the father-gap as well as it can possibly be filled by any human being other than a father.

And that is why the one thing I want to do in the time I have remaining until I drop is to educate people that we're in a battle. The devil is trying to steal the destinies of all these fatherless young men. When my dad died, I knew the devil wanted to step into that place—that weak place—and put up a beachhead there for his evil operations in my life. Every fatherless boy faces the same challenge.

I had a dream once of a jump ball on a basketball court, with the devil on one side and the Lord on the other. The kids of this generation were the ball, up for grabs.

What will we do with these boys?

Jesus once asked, "What father, if his son asks for bread, gives him a rock?" No sane father hands out stones. But the boys I'm concerned about don't even have dads, and they certainly don't deserve rocks. We can't take the place of their fathers, nor can Team Focus put back in their lives what is impossible to restore. When you choose to step into a boy's life, you will not fill the father space, so don't even try. But you *can* do something practical to help. Here's what it will cost you:

1. Talk

You won't have to do much more than this. Our sincere words carry great healing, and if we can speak such words into the wound of a boy, it can be powerful medicine.

But you also need to listen! Spend time listening to a boy. Don't think that every conversation you have with him has to be serious—and *please*, don't make him talk about his dad every time you get together. But as you get to know each other and the walls come down, he will need a listening ear. Be ready.

These boys are forced to make decisions, both important ones and not-so-important ones, without having the information and experience that normally comes from a father. When you're young and trying to figure out life for yourself, it's hard. Having someone else to talk to, to help you along and come into your life at those points of decision, makes a huge difference.

2. *Truth*

As I have said, I always tell the guys in Team Focus, "It's not going to get good, but it's going to get better every day. It's a slow process, but you're going to mend, you're going to heal. Every day you're going to get better. You're never going to get over it and you will never understand the loss of your father— but it's going to get better."

If I told them it *can* get as good as new and that they could eventually forget their dad's absence and reach a place when they would no longer feel any hurt or loss or grief, it would be a complete and utter lie. And it would significantly damage their future.

Speaking these kinds of false platitudes, especially in the name of God, creates faulty expectations. And when they come up empty, a young man can easily think that somehow God didn't come through for him, that God hasn't kept His promise.

Instead, we can offer hope beyond the pain. We can help demonstrate that life doesn't have to be perfect in to find one's God-given destiny.

The young people of today have sensitive "truth detectors" that continually scan the people in their lives to see if those folks are speaking honestly. Be prepared to be honest! At some point it may become appropriate to let a kid know some of the pain from your experience. Ask God to help you recognize when that time arrives and then to have the wisdom to know what to say (and what not to say).

3. Time

I cannot be more certain about one thing: you will never be a stand-in for a father unless you take the time to do it. The five father-factors we've already considered do not happen in a minute.

There is no such thing as speedy acceptance; it takes significant effort to make a boy know he is loved.

You can't come up to a near stranger, give him a hug, and hope that it means anything. A relationship that welcomes affection takes time to nurture.

There is no such thing as "convenient attention," and hasty authority will always breed rebellion instead of supplying protection.

Affirmation can happen in a moment, but it becomes most effective only when backed up by a relationship.

These three elements—talk, truth, and time—are the mechanisms for the best application of the father-functions. To step into the life of a boy who has no dad and expect to fill the gap, you must be willing to make a commitment to each of these elements. And if you do so, you will not only fill a void in a boy's heart, you will find your own life changed.

That, I promise.

CHAPTER TEN

THE WORK
OF TEAM FOCUS

The purpose of Team Focus is to try to put into the lives of boys what their fathers aren't there to provide. We don't take the place of fathers; as I've repeatedly said, nobody can do that. But we try to fill the gap.

Team Focus exists to help fill that gap with good people and good things. We want to step into the picture of a young life and do what we can to fill the hole left by a missing dad. Some dads are missing for good; they've died or they've abandoned the family or are in prison for life. They won't be back. Other fathers are AWOL. They're out of the picture simply because they've stopped being functional fathers. They just don't care enough to be around.

At Team Focus we tell the boys all the time, "We can't be

your dad. We can't replace him and we don't even want to. But we'll try to help fill the gap. We love you and care about you. We'll hang tough. You can count on us."

It's a promise we intend to keep.

■

Destinies don't show up overnight, like milk bottles on a porch. The idea that God might want to use me to start a ministry— an organization reaching out to hundreds of boys across the country who don't have dads—didn't spring up one day out of the blue. No prophet came to my home to deliver a message from on high. The ministry didn't come to me in a dream, although I've had dreams about the ministry. Instead, God worked slowly over the years to prepare my heart for His plans. He unfolded the plan the way a football team unfolds a win: one play at a time.

Some moments on the field of my life brought rough plays that laid me out cold: my father's death, Marcy's difficult birth, my firing from Pitt. Other moments seemed to play out like clockwork: the early father-influencers, my meeting and marrying Mickey, God's gift of two wonderful girls, and the many friends who have blessed me over the years. God has used the hard moments as teaching opportunities to get me into position for this present season. The good times have been a refreshing drink, offering just what I needed at just the right time.

In that way, the job at ESPN set me up for the next play in God's game plan.

I felt restless in Mobile, but I didn't know what to do about it. Mickey, with her God-given insight, noticed what was going on and sensed what I needed. She'd also been clued in by God that something big was up—God himself was going in a "new direction," and this time I would go along.

One evening in 1993, as Mickey and I got ready to go out for dinner, we were having that familiar pre-meal-out discussion so many married couples know so well: "Where do you want to go?" "I don't know, where do you want to go?" "I don't have anywhere in mind, you pick." "I don't have anywhere either, so what are you hungry for?" "I can't decide, I want you to pick for me." "How about Applebee's, then?" "No, I don't want that."

You get the idea.

In the middle of our discussion, something occurred to Mickey. She felt frustrated with the back-and-forth of the conversation and even more frustrated with my restlessness. Out of the blue, she said, "Let's go pick up two boys and take them to eat with us." She figured that if we were going to spend thirty dollars on a meal, maybe we could go to a place for half the price and take some guys along. Besides, I often did this with friends and relatives, just as my dad once had. But she had suggested a couple of unknown boys.

"What boys?" I asked. We didn't know any boys, so I didn't get what she was suggesting.

"I don't know who, but I know that somewhere in the city

of Mobile, there are a couple of boys sitting on the front stoop of their house, bored and ready to get into trouble—and if we took them to dinner, maybe they wouldn't."

Mickey wasn't thinking of any two guys in particular. Instead, she saw something with the eyes of her heart. In a subtle way, God was using Mickey to plant a seed.

I replied with an unequivocal "No!" I had effectively pulled away from the public eye and had no interest in going out of my way to pull some needy boys into my life. "I don't feel like doing that. *No.*"

But I soon learned Mickey was talking about more than just a meal, more than just an investment of dinner. She was talking about our lives. We were sitting on our time, on the extra hours and days God had granted us because of my job. When she made her suggestion that night, Mickey was really saying, "Look. We have the funds and we have the time. Maybe we should share some of that with someone who needs it, like boys in Mobile? Maybe we should be doing more than we're doing."

I admit I was being selfish. After all those years making football teams the center of my life, now I had a chance to be with my family, enjoy the good life, not be so busy, and not feel obligated to meet anyone's needs but my own.

On the other hand, I was doing a lot of moping around, feeling sorry for myself that I wasn't coaching. I felt washed-up. Put out to pasture. Set on the shelf.

That night we didn't scour the neighborhoods of Mobile looking for a couple of kids who wanted a hamburger. But God had planted a seed, deep down in the soil of my heart—soil that God had been working over for many years to get just right for that very moment. This was the first time I felt my Lord tug at me to wake me up, to let me know that, just maybe, I needed to spend time with some boys with histories like my own—boys without dads. I had grown hard inside, and so it took time, but the seed eventually started to sprout and grow.

Sometimes we fight what God is trying to do in our lives. Don't make that mistake! If you don't answer the call, eventually He's going to call somebody else. The incident that evening was God's way of getting my attention and pointing my heart in a specific direction. I had little interest in moving that way, but already the game plan was changing. Despite my initial resistance, God's seed planting would bear fruit. I had no way of knowing it, but God was even then at work to fund the harvest.

The Web site for the GMAC Bowl describes its official history like this:

> All great things begin with a degree of daydreaming. A simple idea soon becomes a constant thought. Then, when mentioned in random conversation, the idea explodes into action.
>
> Stan Tiner, former editor of the Mobile Register, is the man who first uttered the "What if" scenario

in reference to the bowl game being played today. Tiner, a long-time supporter of sports in Mobile, discussed the possibilities of an NCAA-sanctioned bowl game with Mobile Mayor Mike Dow for the first time in 1998, and Dow immediately saw the possibilities.

With phrases such as economic impact, national exposure *and* hotel occupancy *dancing in their heads, Tiner and Dow looked within the city for help and approached the former University of Pittsburgh head coach and longtime resident of the Port City, Mike Gottfried, for leadership and direction.*

Gottfried, using his contacts as a former head coach and now college football analyst for ESPN, as well as his established friendships within college athletics circles, assessed the city's efforts and began to build support for attracting a bowl game in Mobile. Almost immediately, the City of Mobile and mayor got behind the project.

When Mike Dow, mayor of Mobile, asked me if it would be feasible or desirable to bring a bowl game to Mobile, I had no good answer for him. So he challenged me to find the answer.

Since I was still trying to dodge the eye of the public, however, privately I told Mickey, "I don't know about being involved in a bowl game. I've enjoyed my time, I'm enjoying the girls, and we're out from under the pressure."

I met with Mike and Stan anyway, and they asked if I

would research the inner workings of bowl games. They wanted to bring two teams together at the end of the season that came from either the Western Athletic Conference, the Mid-American Conference, or Conference USA. My task was to visit cities with existing bowl games, talk to the organizers, and find out all I could about the games and how a city gets involved. They knew I could make the contacts and get the appointments necessary, so I reluctantly agreed to do just that much—but I made it clear, that was it. I would help them conduct a feasibility investigation, but then I was done.

I flew to Detroit and met with George Perles and the Motor City Bowl people. Next I traveled to Arizona and talked to the Fiesta Bowl guys. After that, it was the Independence Bowl and Peach Bowl. When I had finished, I returned to Mobile to meet with Mike and Stan.

"Okay, fellas, this can work," I said. "We can do this." I didn't want to admit it, but I was getting pretty excited about the whole project.

After two years of further research and development, we met with a team of organizers to begin finalizing the plans. I had finished my research—that's all I had promised to do—but now, the circle of people climbing on board was expanding. The organizing committee asked if I would take the plunge and get personally involved. I began to see there might be more to the whole idea than just a game. When sponsors expressed interest in chipping in, I realized how we could use the bowl game to give back to the community—a significant contribution, in fact. So I made my continued participation contingent on that factor.

"I'll get involved with this bowl game on one condition," I told the group, "that we make sure we give something back to the community of Mobile." They agreed, so I went further. "I'm setting the goal of raising fifty thousand dollars, free and clear after the game has been paid for. We can use that money around the city in all kinds of ways." They loved the idea.

Working with the bowl president, Jerry Silverstein, I sometimes put in eighteen-hour days assembling the plans. Jerry and I and the rest of the team wanted to make sure we pulled the first bowl game off without a hitch, because we knew that if it was to have any future, the coaches, players, fans, and media would all have to give it a thumbs-up.

We held our first bowl game in 1999. The city sponsored it the first year, calling it the Mobile Bowl. It was a rousing success! The second year, GMAC came on as our sponsor. We raised the money for the bowl, plus the money we had budgeted as a gift to Mobile—and then we started to spend it.

That money was like fishes and loaves. We spread it as far as we could, and yet we still had more to give away. We looked at the groups and places in Mobile that were really helping people and making a difference in the lives of the disadvantaged. We wanted agencies and ministries that directly helped those who most needed it. We wanted to invest in them.

We gave some money to the local Ronald McDonald house and some to the Boys and Girls Clubs of Mobile. I also wanted to use the funds for other charities that, although they lacked a high profile, were really making a difference in Mobile—organizations such as Our Sisters' Closet, a ministry offering clothing to mothers. By the time we were done, we had given away thirty-five thousand dollars to more than fifteen Mobile area charities . . . but we still had fifteen thousand dollars left. We couldn't believe it.

Mickey and I looked at the records and the balance sheet after calculating what we'd given away. "What are we going to do with the rest of that money?" I asked. Mickey didn't hesitate. She answered fresh from her heart: "We'll start a camp for boys." So we started brainstorming.

"What boys should come?" Mickey asked.

"There are a lot of services available to at-risk kids already."

"Right. So who needs help?"

"What about boys without dads? Boys like me."

It was like a puzzle piece that fit only one way, and we'd found it, sitting in our hearts, just waiting to slip into the perfect picture of God's plan. We had a great desire to aim for a boy with an empty space in his family picture, a boy who needed a stand-in dad. We pictured that boy in our heads.

"He's sitting at home, lonely. He needs a mentor, an adult to say, 'Good job!' He could be white, black, Hispanic—doesn't matter. His mom loves him, but she can't be a dad to him."

"Right. And he needs someone to pat him on the shoulder or give him a hug."

"And tell him he belongs, make him feel like part of the

family. This boy doesn't have anybody who will show him he's valuable. And he needs someone who cares enough to hold him accountable."

"And if he doesn't get someone in his life to help fill that space, it's gonna be filled by all the wrong things."

Our thoughts came pouring out, like a dam bursting inside our hearts. That dam had held back those thoughts for a long time, but the moment had at last come for the dream to stream out of our heads and into reality.

"Okay. So, how do we find him? Where is that boy?"

"We'll look at the schools, the charities, the churches." We had good connections all over town: we knew the school superintendent, some pastors, and other civic leaders. "But what will we do when we find them?"

"We'll invite them to a camp. At the camp we'll do the things a dad does. We'll help them learn to fish, teach them to balance a checkbook, show them how to tie a tie, and be courteous." We just kept talking. And there, at the kitchen counter, a dream spilled out and turned into a river of life for fatherless boys.

Now I was excited! I had found something I didn't know I was looking for, something special, something more. I needed something that would match my passion and capture my long-term attention. Down deep, I wanted something I could tackle head-on and get excited about.

This was it.

I returned to the bowl officials and said, "I've figured out a plan for the leftover money. Let me have that money to start a camp for boys without dads." They agreed, we made the plans and scheduled the camp, and Team Focus was born. About sixty boys joined us for our first ever Team Focus camp, and most of them are still with us.

◼

For our first camp, held in 2000, we set an age limit of nine to sixteen. One boy, Jim, had his little brother, Parker, standing in line with him to register for camp. Parker looked a little sad. I saw the two of them and asked Parker, "How old are you?"

"I'm seven, sir."

"Okay," I said, "you and your mom go home and get your stuff and come back. You can come, too." So both brothers came to camp. I've let a lot of younger boys into the program over the years, but I've been told to lay off my invitations to kids younger than nine—they have a hard time keeping up with the pace at camp.

That first camp, we couldn't understand hardly anything Jim said. He mumbled when he talked and he was painfully shy. Jim's still a little shy, but he became our first high school graduate. Now he's a student at the University of South Alabama, majoring in electrical engineering and maintaining a 3.57 GPA. His goal is to own his own business.

A quiet, angry middle schooler named Randall also came to the first Camp Focus. He had a rough and tough look, with chains around his neck and attitude on his face. It was obvious that he thrived on negative attention. Randall's dad was in prison, so Randall got shuttled back and forth between his mom and aunt. All of his brothers had been in trouble, and Randall was heading the same way. But he loved the camp and turned things around. He's been with Team Focus ever since, and now he helps us with the other camps. Randall is a senior in high school and plays football.

Davis attended the first camp, too. During registration, Davis's mom waited in the corner while I got some last-minute things done. Mickey noticed that Mrs. Davis kept waiting, obviously hoping to talk to me and clearly concerned about something important. The poor lady waited quite a while, and finally Mickey drew my attention to her.

"Is there anything we can do for you?" I asked.

She looked intently at Mickey and me. "Yes, sir. I want you to take care of my boy."

I figured she felt anxious about leaving Davis in the care of complete strangers—a justifiable concern. "Don't worry," I replied, "he'll have a great week."

Mickey chimed in, "Oh, he's going to have a great week here. He's going to be just fine."

Mrs. Davis just shook her head and answered, "No, you don't understand what I'm saying. I want you to take care of him." Again we tried to assure her that everything would be fine and Davis would be taken care of. Finally she made her good-byes and we got busy with the camp.

It took six months for us to understand what she really meant. That's when Davis's mom died. Since then, Mickey and I have become involved personally in Davis's life; we remain close to him. We've tried to honor his mother's request.

Incidents like these show me that God really did have a plan, not for harm, but for good. Just as He promised, it was a plan for a hope and a future—it just took me a long time to get it. Finally I understood that God intends that hope and future not only for me, but for boys just like me who ache for the loss of a father. Those are the boys my heart has always been drawn to. And those are the boys we try to reach through Team Focus.

We scheduled our first camp at South Alabama University for five days. Then we began gathering some help from former players and coaches I'd worked with, as well as others from GMAC or the bowl. We ended up with ten staffers. We garnered the names of boys from several city referrals, and sixty of them said they were coming.

But what were we going to do with them?

Today, I marvel that *any* mothers or grandmothers sent us their boys. We had no reputation, no track record. We had nothing to prove that we could help a boy. When a couple of the moms and grandmas came to register their boys, they asked us, "You don't get anything for free. What's the catch?" They couldn't figure out why we weren't collecting any money. They'd never heard of Team Focus, and most of them had never heard of me. It was easy for them to be suspicious, and I didn't blame them. On the surface, it must have been easy to conclude, *There's something wrong with this.* But amazingly, they sent sixty of their sons, anyway.

It's funny, but this original camp was not supposed to be the first one. It was supposed to be the only one. In fact, we hadn't thought about anything beyond that first camp. We had the extra money from the bowl game and the remainder from what we'd given away. Those funds would pay for one camp, with a little left over. So we planned one camp, for one time, in one city. We had no other plans.

But as my life has proved over and over, God's plans are higher, deeper, and better than mine.

In the middle of that first camp, we saw something happen that opened our eyes and gave us a bit of God's perspective. We saw something that started small, but had huge potential. As the week progressed, all of us marveled at what God was doing. We really were in awe. Our sponsors from GMAC saw the potential, took the idea back to the company, and GMAC has been a major funding source ever since.

Honestly, we didn't even want to look at what was happening. We didn't want to talk about the potential or admit what was going on, because we all knew what it meant. It was like a train leaving the roundhouse and heading out for destinations unknown. We were trying to catch up to it—to the idea, the momentum—and it was building up steam, chugging and churning and taking off, moving faster and faster. The whole thing was a much bigger idea than any of us had imagined . . . and it was rolling.

This is big, we thought. *This is really big.*

As we built the program, we talked about all the things a boy learns from his father. Most of those things can't be taught in a book. Many of those things can't even be explained—a boy just has to have someone in his life who can live it out in front of him, so he can see how it's done.

I made a list of all the things I missed out on after Dad died, then we incorporated those things into Team Focus camps— such things as tying a tie, fishing, manners. Practical things such as how to pick clothes to wear, or how to eat in a nice restaurant, or how to study. Prickly topics such as relationships, purity, and how to ask a girl out on a date. We tried to think of everything.

Can a mom teach these things to a boy? Sure. A mom can help tie a tie, bait a hook, or balance a checkbook—but not in the same way as a dad. And most single moms are swamped. They struggle to earn a living and raise a family and cover all the bases that, in an intact family, a dad would help to cover. Single moms just don't have the time and energy to do everything.

But really, it goes beyond all that. When I watch sixty boys attempting to put a necktie into shape around their neck, I'm not watching a tie-tying lesson. They probably think that's what's happening, but it's not the main thing; it's not the lasting, important thing. If those boys never learned to tie a tie, it wouldn't be the end of the world. In the same way, when I see sixty boys at the edge of a lake, with sixty fishing poles wagging in the air and sixty lines flying into the water and sixty hooks lodging into the bushes and trees and human flesh around that lake, I'm not looking at a fishing class. If those boys never learned to fish, they'd probably make it.

But let me tell you something. When you watch sixty boys, surrounded by men, many of whom have father-gaps of their own, and those men are laughing with them, shouting at them, telling them "Nice cast!" or "You look sharp!" or "That's okay, we'll get it, why don't you try again?"—that's where the action takes place. That's where the real business is getting done. And that's what Team Focus is all about.

It's great when a boy catches his first fish—what a thrill! And to see a bunch of guys get dressed up in shirts and ties, all of them knowing they look *fine*—well, it's satisfying.

But to hear a boy who has never shared his story with anyone finally open up and tell about how it is to watch your dad get killed on your front porch, then to have men gather around that boy and hug him and pray with him and let his tears fall—let me tell you, *God is in that moment.*

■

Neckties and learning to tie them have become a kind of symbol for Team Focus. We land in a lot of newspapers around the country with stories of tying ties, complete with pictures. We've received donations of ties, some new and some from executive wardrobes, and we try to find a generous source for clothing so each boy can have a brand-new, button-down dress shirt.

You have yet to really live unless you've been in a room full of sixty or seventy boys with ties flying and men running around helping!

Some of the boys balk at first. "I'm never going to wear a tie," they say, so they don't need to learn. Some just aren't excited about another guy's castoffs. But I tell you what, they *love* it when they learn. We have the older boys, who've already learned, teach the younger ones, like big brothers in the same family.

It's true that some dads never teach their sons to tie a necktie, and yet they're still great fathers. But learning how to do it gives our boys a sense of pride, of success. It helps them understand what is necessary in the business world. It opens their eyes to their own value. You should see the looks on their faces when they see themselves in a mirror wearing a nice dress shirt and a tie, some of them for the first time. And they've tied that knot all by themselves!

They feel good about themselves. They feel special. You might even say they feel blessed.

That's also why, on the final evening of our camps, we believe in giving the boys a blessing—speaking God's blessing over them. This is something that a father would do, or at least should do, for his children. When a son has a birthday, a good father might stand behind his boy before cutting the birthday cake and pray a blessing, thanking God for the gift of this child and asking God to bless this young life. That's something these boys never get, so we take care of that at camp.

Each boy comes up and Pastor Rey places his hands on every one and prays. Rey has a spiritual sense of the destiny of these kids, and he prays God's will for them. He commends their talents and expresses gratefulness for each boy. He asks

God to heal the hurts of a missing father. In that moment of blessing, he applies all the father-functions at once: affection, attention, affirmation, authority, and acceptance.

And in that holy moment, at the intersection of past pain and future hope, God shows up. Tears flow. Lives get altered. Choices are made.

I think my dad likes what he sees.

The boys in Team Focus need to know that someone in their lives empathizes with their pain. That's why many of the people I have brought in to help me have "been there" themselves. They've lost their own dad at a young age, so they can relate to the boys.

On many occasions when men have come to help or observe what we do at Team Focus, God has picked that moment to make their own walls of self-protection come tumbling down. One leader in his midforties came into camp as a volunteer, along with his wife. At the awards banquet, when we speak solemnly to the boys about their hurt and about what God can do in their lives, this man broke down and wept. He admitted it was the first time he had ever allowed himself to feel the hurt of his own heart.

His father had abandoned him when he was a child, and he had never taken the time to grieve over his loss. Instead, he had built up a strong wall of self-protection. At camp, God moved into that hard area of his heart and softened it so that healing could begin. He came to camp because of a genuine desire to help Team Focus. He left it finally able to come to terms with what had happened in his own life, so many years before.

God is working all over this ministry, and that's why we want to keep walking through any open door he brings our way.

From the beginning, Team Focus has been a seat-of-your-pants kind of operation, and we still keep moving forward in that way. Even now the train keeps rolling, and we haven't caught up with it yet.

Team Focus camps have been held in Washington, D.C.; San Diego; Detroit; Mobile; Ashland, Ohio; Los Angeles; and other cities. We hold them mostly on college campuses, but sometimes in hotels or retreat and conference centers. This year we will add more cities to the list and more boys to the program.

We currently have more than one thousand boys who have attended a Team Focus camp and who stay in communication with us. At our office, our guidance counselor, Christy, keeps tabs on all the boys and their progress. She stays in contact with the schools the boys attend, and she helps with their testing and college admissions.

Cathy Nabors, our office manager, does a remarkable job with all the details: scheduling, organizing, and communications. Regional directors such as Rocky Alt, Bill Hubans, Keith Howard, and Pat Adams stay in contact with the boys in their respective areas and plan various activities with them. I know the boys by name, keep their information with me in an ever-expanding notebook, and they all have my cell phone number. I turn it off only when I'm on the air.

While that may sound organized, it has grown only as God has directed. We continue to depend on Him for the future. We had no blueprint or template to figure out how to do it, we just knew that *this* was what we needed to do. And we've moved ahead as God has opened the doors.

Every day we want to trust God for the challenges of the new day. The boys come to us in various stages of brokenness, from all kinds of situations beyond our control. But God gives us what we need for that moment to offer the most help we possibly can, to fill the void with good things, not evil.

Today we can look back and see clearly that God has been guiding and directing every step of the way. Like so many of God's workings in the lives of people through the ages, we have determined to trust Him and move through the doors and windows as He opens them—and He has honored our faith.

Last year we had a rally in Mobile, Alabama, in which we brought in more than two hundred of our guys from around the country. We wanted to get them all together so they could see they were not alone, but were part of a large group of boys in the same boat, facing the same challenges, and getting some significant wins. Flying them all into Mobile and seeing them together in one place gave us a picture of what the future holds for us, although I'm not in charge of that. God is.

As I said, those plans are in His hands, just like His plans for my life. Whatever His plans may be for Team Focus, I don't get too concerned about it. I don't focus on the money. The leadership of the ministry makes decisions on what the boys need and what will be best for the group, and we consider the money to be God's business. We don't wait for it to come in; we just trust that God will lead us. If He's leading, then He'll provide. We don't have a surplus, but we have what we need.

I sometimes get the question "What about the girls? Girls who don't have dads need this, too." And that's absolutely correct.

Girls who grow up without a dad are desperate for male attention. The statistics for girls without dads are just as alarming as those for boys. I think it would be great if a ministry could focus its attention on those girls, and I pray for someone to step up to that calling. But God put a passion in me to come alongside boys without fathers, to help plug the hole.

Remember, that's what I liked best about being a coach, working with the guys. I grew to love them, to care about their lives and concerns. Between my love for the game and my love of the players, I could have stayed in coaching my whole life. But in coaching, especially coaching big teams from big schools with big programs, other stuff got in the way. Today I choose to push that stuff aside to give more time to a boy without a dad.

When I was recruiting, I seemed to have a second sense about whether a boy was fatherless. If the dad wasn't around, I could see it, feel it. I'd be tactful and say something like "Will your dad be joining us?" or "I'd like to meet your father sometime," and they'd tell me, "I don't have a father." I'd make a mental note to take a little extra care of that one; I knew what he was going through. It was like an inner magnet that allowed me to find the emptiness and come alongside to help. The empty father shape inside me gave me a sensitivity to others who shared the same hole.

I know what such young men are thinking and feeling. I've walked where they walk. Times have changed, of course, and we live in a much more complicated world than I did; but I can still understand them, appreciate their pain and loss, and grasp the hole in their lives left by an absent dad.

The progress we've seen in our boys makes all of our efforts worth everything we've put into it. Four of the boys who began with us are now graduating from high school and starting college. Peyton is our first to enter the military; he's in Iraq. By the time you read this, we'll have several more boys out of high school and starting the next phase of their futures.

We have no intention of stepping out of their lives. We are trusting God to show us what to do next that will be most helpful to them as they move on through college and into careers. Team Focus continues to move out as the boys grow up. I didn't plan on it, but we keep adding and growing.

Jake Peavy, a pitcher with the San Diego Padres, has helped with some of our events in Mobile. He once told me, "Mike, we want to have this program in San Diego. We need Team

Focus down there." We listened to his counsel and followed through on it last summer. And that's the way the ministry has grown.

We look for God working ahead of us. At one staff retreat, we attempted to come up with a plan for the future, to set an agenda about where we will go, how we should expand. A lot of people want us to come to their city, so how do we choose?

Above all, we look for passion. When we see God moving in the hearts of people and stirring them to work, we take notice. When we see people getting on board and moving forward, we feel we can move in alongside to help.

After I spoke at a church in Las Vegas, some men there talked to me about having Team Focus there. As they described how many homeless boys lived in their city, their passion about the boys became clear. They had already begun planning and meeting needs. God is already working there! And if God's already moving there, that's where we want to go.

This is the ministry the Lord gave to Mickey and me. To the best of our ability, we're doing things the way God wants them done. As I said, right now we have more than one thousand boys involved in Team Focus. We're aiming for ten times that amount—six thousand boys. I don't know who they are or where they live. I don't know how we'll pull it off, and I don't know how we'll pay for it all. I don't know if I can memorize all six thousand names.

But with God's help, I'm gonna give it a try.

FILL THE GAP

Do you know the most powerful change that takes place in a boy's life when he loses his dad? Fear. Fear moves in, and all of a sudden the happy life he once had gets wrenched away.

He doesn't know how his mom will look out for him. The future is gone, forever altered. Somehow a thief came and stole his father, leaving him vulnerable and exposed. As good as his mom can be, he feels as though some of his protection has been stripped away. He feels like easy prey. His confidence is shot.

Do you know what the five father-functions do? They restore confidence. When a boy receives any of these in a genuine, loving fashion, a little confidence builds up. When a boy finds a man who can take up some of these functions, his confidence level can grow strong and healthy once more.

I doubt I need to convince you that fatherlessness is a problem for any child, and especially for boys. But I also want you to know that not having a father does not seal the fate of a boy, dooming him to a drug problem or an educational disaster or a jail sentence. The clear fact is that a boy without a dad *can* make it. Not only can he succeed, but he can thrive in this world, grow up strong in the Lord, and become the person God intended from the beginning. He can best accomplish these things, however, only if the hole left by his father in the family picture gets filled by others who will retrofit the five father-functions into the gap.

So what can you do? Help to fill the gap.

* If you are a woman, encourage a reliable man in your life to help out.

* If you are a man, choose to step into the life of a fatherless boy and stand in for a dad.

However you choose to help fill this gap, keep in mind the five father-functions for which every boy cries out. For one last time, may I remind you of each one?

1. Affection
Touch a boy today! I understand that we live in an unsafe world and that we have to be careful and discerning in the way we show affection. But we dare not let caution stop us from offering appropriate touch to boys. An arm around a shoulder, a pat on the back, or a big bear hug will say what words can never convey, especially when that hug is offered by another man who cares about that boy like a dad.

2. Attention
Give a boy your notice. Let him be in your sights. Watch what's going on in his life and show interest in him. Learn about who he is and what his interests are. Go with him to a game, teach him to tie a tie or to fish. Take him along to work with you.

3. Affirmation
Let your words and your actions provide solid evidence for hope. Ask yourself, "What can I say and do to help a fatherless

boy know there is hope for him? What words can I offer, what encouragement can I bring, and what actions can I take that will assure him he has a future and that he can pursue his dreams?" Then speak those words and do those things. Affirm the destiny of a fatherless boy!

4. Authority

If you're in a position to offer this kind of function in a boy's life, take it seriously. You may be a teacher or a pastor. You might be a church-club leader or a neighbor. Working with the permission and active guidance of the boy's mom or guardian, you can help set boundaries and provide safety for a young man swimming alone in the sea of contemporary temptation— a dangerous place to be without a rudder. Be the rudder.

5. Acceptance

With Mom's permission and help, invite a boy to share in your family life. Bring him along on family outings. Invite him to dinner with you and your wife and kids. Expose him to what an intact family is like. Show him your unconditional love.

This may be an intimidating and even daunting list, but don't let it blow you away! Take just one or two things and begin to work on them. It's not hard and you don't need any special abilities and training.

But you do need one thing: you have to make a commitment! What a fatherless boy emphatically *does not need* is another man making empty promises and worthless excuses. If you're going to fill the gap, decide right now that you are not going to give up. Make a decision that you are going to hang in there and be a part of this kid's life from now on. Period.

If you really want to help fill the gap, it's the only way.

A FATHER'S BLESSING

've been to Congress many times, mostly as an advocate for fatherless boys.

A few years ago I made an appointment with my congressman, Mr. Jo Bonner. I wanted to acquaint him with the ministry of Team Focus, especially in Mobile, the largest city he represents. It didn't take long to realize I'd made a solid connection. As I explained our programs and described our kids, he knew exactly what I was talking about. I could see it in his eyes, which began to well up with tears. It turned out we'd both grown up without a dad.

"I lost my own dad when I was eleven," he told me. "I vividly remember the first time I tried to tie a necktie after he died. It was that one action—in that moment—that the reality hit me in a powerful, emotional way. *My dad would never be back*. He would never be there to help me tie my ties again. I cried."

As you know by now, tying a tie is an issue for me, too. And from that visit on, Team Focus had an advocate with Jo Bonner.

Jo set up our meeting with Laura Bush's team. The first lady has a real interest in helping fatherless boys, one that doesn't get a lot of media attention. Jo arranged our White House meeting so that we could describe our ministry to boys.

Jo told us, "You'll probably have ten, maybe fifteen minutes, max. Just be ready with fifteen minutes of your best information."

Since I wanted my best team with me, my wife, Mickey, joined me. I also brought along Marshall Banks, a distinguished member of our board of directors.

Just before we entered the White House, you may remember, one of my boys called me on my cell phone. No emergency, no pressing need for advice. He just wanted to check in. But when he heard what we were about to do, he asked a great question that I asked you to ponder at the beginning of this book. Here it is again:

What are you doing here?

Now that you've read my story, learned something about Team Focus and why we exist, and heard my challenge to fill the gap for at least one fatherless boy, can you understand why I think it's such a crucial question? For a long time, I didn't really know how to answer it. After I lost my coaching job at Pitt, especially, I had no clear idea of what I was doing on this planet. I thought it was just my time to kick back, enjoy some anonymity for a change, and take care of my family and myself.

But as you also know by now, God had other plans for me!

Today, I know exactly why I'm here. God has shaped my life, molded my circumstances, and directed my steps so that I am in a prime position to minister to fatherless boys. And to be real honest, that makes me wonder, *Could it be that God has directed you to this very book so that you, too, can step into the life of some young man who lacks a functioning father?*

I don't know what "filling the gap" might look like for you. Nor can I say what you ought to do next. Only God knows those things, and only God has the wisdom to direct you where you need to be. Often, though, I've noticed that He moves us to exactly the right spot simply by asking questions. And so I think once again of the question currently on the table:

What are you doing here?

The fact that I still miss my dad deeply helps me to answer that question with clarity, passion, and certainty. I don't know how you'd answer the question, but I pray that if you don't yet have a good answer in mind, you will have one soon.

Let me leave you with something special that you might not expect from a former college football coach. I'm still thinking about my dad these days, and I think a lot about what I'd like to say to him if he were here, or what I'd like to do with him. I put those thoughts into a poem.

A FATHER'S BLESSING

Dad:
Let's play catch
Go for a walk
Go together to a game

Put your hand on my shoulder
Give me that look of approval
Give me a hug and a kiss

Tell me you love me
Tell me I am special
Tell me you're proud of me
Tell me I'm yours

Give me your blessing, Dad
I really need it!
Give me your love—Cover me with your love

Thanks, Dad!

CHALLENGED, ENCOURAGED, MOTIVATED.

Team Focus is a comprehensive community and outreach program founded by Mike and Mickey Gottfried. A young man without a father figure in his life cries out for affirmation. A father affirms a child, builds character, and gives him self-esteem, worth, and confidence. We provide these young men with role models and positive influences that can impact their lives now and in the future. Mike's vision and drive for the program is based on his life experiences.

For more information visit www.teamfocusonline.org